RYAN'S LUCK

A LIFE OF PETER RYAN MM

John Tidey is a Melbourne journalist and author. His newspaper memoir *Stories From A Bygone Age* was published in 2018. He is married to Jackie, a writer and publisher of books for children.

Books by John Tidey

Stories from a Bygone Age: A Newspaper Memoir
Class Act: A Life of Creighton Burns
One of a Kind: The Life of Charles Hastings Barton (with Ric Barton)
The Big Sheppartonian: A Life of Sir Andrew Fairley
Developing Tomorrow's Newspaper Managers (with Rick Knowles)

RYAN'S LUCK

A LIFE OF PETER RYAN MM

JOHN TIDEY

ARCADIA

First published 2020 by Arcadia
the general books imprint of
Australian Scholarly Publishing Ltd
7 Lt Lothian St Nth, North Melbourne, Vic 3051
Tel: 03 9329 6963 / Fax: 03 9329 5452
enquiry@scholarly.info / www.scholarly.info

ISBN 978-1-922454-09-6 (Paperback)

ISBN 978-1-922454-08-9 (Hardback)

Cover design: Wayne Saunders

For Jackie, Sarah and Nick.

CONTENTS

Acknowledgements *ix*

Preface *xi*

Acronyms *xii*

1 Scholarship Boy 1

2 Courage and Betrayal 15

3 Winding Road Ahead 40

4 A Real Bookman 63

5 Much More to Do 96

Postscript 121

Appendices

My Tallest Adventure *123*

Evening by the Sea *126*

Selected Sources *127*

Works by Peter Ryan *130*

Index *131*

ACKNOWLEDGEMENTS

It would have been much more difficult to research and write this life of Peter Ryan without the assistance of his daughter, Sally Guerin and his son Andrew Ryan. Both of them were enthusiastic supporters of the project from the start. Sally Guerin is the keeper of what might be called the Peter Ryan Archive at her home in Melbourne. This is a vast array of letters, pictures, files and clippings, books and brochures, as well as his World War Two medals and official documents from his long life. It also includes Ryan's carefully assembled *Guard Books* as he called them; a newspaper reporter would call them *Scrapbooks.* Whatever you call them they were immensely useful. Sally was very generous with her time and in sharing her knowledge of her father's life. Andrew Ryan, who lives in country New South Wales, provided many anecdotes and pieces of family background that helped in the presentation of his father. I am very grateful to both of them. Their mother, Davey Ryan, was delighted the book was being written.

This is an opportunity to acknowledge my former newspaper industry colleague John Farquharson (1929–2016) and his valuable four-hour interview with Peter Ryan recorded in October 2000. It was undertaken for the Oral History Section of the National Library of Australia. The one-hour interview video in 2009 with

Peter Ryan by Reg Yates, dealing mainly with Papua New Guinea issues, was also helpful. The Royal Australian Artillery History Company helped me sort out a couple of issues related to Ryan's early service with the Royal Australian Engineers as a Sapper in anti-aircraft units.

I am particularly grateful for the assistance of Judith Gibson, archivist at Caulfield Grammar School in Melbourne; Madeleine Castles who undertook some research in Canberra during the long months of the Covid crisis when Victorians like the author were not able to leave the state and Melbourne University Press veteran Sue Hardiman. Max Suich went out of his way to help me better understand his friend Peter Ryan. George Thomas and Mike Rosel were generous with their time and skills in helping to get the final manuscript ready. For their contributions large and small, I thank Bernard Teague, Blanche d'Alpuget, Andrew Guerin, Nick Walker, Rowan Callick, Geoffrey Blainey, Michelle Stillman, John Spooner, Nick Tidey, Mark Sheehan, Robert Murray, Alistair Pope, Michael Duffy, Ian Willis, Wendy Sutherland and John Ridley.

My wife Jackie was a constant source of encouragement and advice as this book was researched and written and applied her professional editing skills to the manuscript that emerged. Of course the book would not have appeared at all without the enthusiasm and commitment of the publisher and his team.

PREFACE

When Peter Ryan died one tribute described him as a Universal Man. It was an attractive and far from fanciful view of a brave soldier, respected publisher and brilliant essayist. His achievements were the product of a remarkably complex character: wilfully independent; a man of letters, yet a plain man; a loyal friend but a formidable enemy. At heart he was really a country man, a fine horseman who could strain up a fence and build a house; well, half a house actually. Near the end of his long life it was said that Ryan's eyes were still 'bright with mischief'; ever alert for the next target for his attention.

Peter Ryan saw himself as a *writer* first and foremost. His astonishing output justified such a view: more than two million words (the bulk of them handwritten), maybe 2,000 essays, reviews and articles, nine books and monographs. One admirer declared Ryan incapable of writing an ugly sentence. Another that he was an Australian echo of the English essayist William Hazlitt. His increasingly conservative views meant that he was often off-side in some quarters and a forthright favourite in others. One critic reckoned he was a *cogent, cantankerous, Tory.*

Peter Ryan would have liked that.

ACRONYMS

ADB	Australian Dictionary of Biography
ADO	Assistant District Officer
AFR	*Australian Financial Review*
AIB	Allied Intelligence Bureau
ANGAU	Australian New Guinea Administrative Unit
ANU	Australian National University
ARM	Australian Republican Movement
ASIO	Australian Security Intelligence Organisation
CRA	Conzinc Riotinto of Australia
DFC	Distinguished Flying Cross
DORCA	Directorate of Research and Civil Affairs
FELO	Far Eastern Liaison Office
ICI	Imperial Chemical Industries
ICIANZ	Imperial Chemical Industries of Australia and New Zealand.
MM	Military Medal
MID	Mentioned in Dispatches
MUP	Melbourne University Press
RAE	Royal Australian Engineers
USP	United Service Publicity

I

SCHOLARSHIP BOY

I have taught Peter for five years and have found him outstanding in his general interests. He has a marked gift for literary expression.

Gordon Connell MA, Second Master,
Malvern Church of England Grammar School

It was 1941. If things had gone as Peter Ryan hoped this might have been the year he began his Articles as a future solicitor. Two years earlier he had left school at the end of the Great Depression. Jobs were still hard to find and he was fortunate to get a position as a clerk in the Commonwealth Railways. But it was the law that interested him and he was recruited by Victoria's Crown Law Department where his prospects seemed much brighter. It was a clerical job and the step up to Articles, the path into the legal profession, would require application and some luck. A career in the law beckoned but it would have to wait nearly 50 years. For the next four years Peter Ryan would be a soldier.

World War Two had threatened Australia directly for the first time. It had begun in Europe in 1939 and the war in the Pacific erupted at the end of 1941 drawing the Americans into the conflict. Then, in January 1942, Japanese forces invaded the Australian Territory of New Guinea as hostilities spread through the South West Pacific. Australia had significant responsibilities in the area: it had administered the Territory of New Guinea since 1920. The Territory of Papua—occupying the south-eastern corner of the island of New Guinea—had been placed under the authority of the Commonwealth of Australia back in 1902.

When the Japanese landed in New Guinea Ryan was an 18-year-old soldier in Melbourne and destined to play a small and heroic part in turning back the enemy. Ill prepared, poorly armed and equipped, he would spend months at a time on dangerous intelligence gathering missions behind Japanese lines. It would prove to be the making of him. Years later he would admit that 'Dispatching an eighteen-year-old on such a job as mine was heartless and irresponsible. And yet it was the best thing that ever happened to me. I got the chance to discover what I could do and I am grateful.'

Peter Allen Ryan, the boy who would become a decorated war hero, celebrated writer, publisher—and yes, an Officer of the Supreme Court of Victoria—was born in the family home in suburban Glen Iris, Melbourne, on the fourth of September 1923. There were four boys in the family of Alice and Emmett Ryan: Francis, who died as an infant, Peter, Phillip and Barry. Their mother, Alice Doreen Ryan (*née* Allen), was known as Doreen but to the family she was *Dor Dor*; their father, Emmett, was always 'Ted'. The family home at 27 Glenvale Road was a modest dwelling, one bedroom and one sitting room at the front and a sleep-out in an old-style sunroom at the back where the boys slept. In winter it must have been freezing out there. In the single bathroom a gas burner heated the water above the bath and a sort of widened passage way leading to the kitchen housed a more formal dining area. Vegetables of various kinds filled much of the rear garden area, the backyard. Eighty years after Peter left home to join the army the house he grew up in was still there, clearly recognisable but with a second, modern, storey added. The original stone front fence remained in place.

Peter's brothers were much younger than him: Phillip born in 1929 and Barry in 1931. When Phillip left school he attended Dookie Agricultural College and after years as a stock and station agent was appointed a member of the Rural Finance Commission. Barry, doubtless influenced by the experiences of his father and eldest brother, became a patrol officer in Papua and New Guinea.

At age three young Peter was given a book which he treasured for the rest of his life. It was *A Book for Kids* by C.J. Dennis and the gift of 'Auntie Griff', a friend of Doreen Ryan who had been midwife at Peter's birth. It has now survived its owner, albeit in battered condition. During his long life Peter Ryan amassed 10,000 books and would have read many more. He also collected a diverse range of pamphlets and published speeches, about 300 eventually. From an early age he was a voracious reader: books, comics and that iconic publication of the time, the *Boy's Own Paper* with its tales of endurance, daring and service. Before he was out of his teens he would be undertaking '*Boy's Own*' stuff himself.

The young Ryan—like the adult who emerged—was not much interested, however, in sport as either participant or observer. His poor eyesight would not have helped. 'I scarcely saw a ball before it hit me,' he once explained. His father, Ted, on the other hand, had been an Australian Rules player before World War One, turning out for St Kilda (21 games) and Richmond (12 games). This was a time before footballers were celebrities. They went about their normal lives and work and played club football at the weekend.

It was Ted's stories, his enthusiasm and even the gift of a book to his son that kindled Peter Ryan's lifelong interest in what would become known as Papua New Guinea. Ted was 29 when he joined the army in 1914 and served in the Australian Naval and Military Expeditionary Force. This was a volunteer unit of about 2,000 men sent to capture and occupy German possessions and wireless stations in the New Guinea region. Having done so it provided occupation forces for the rest of the war and Sergeant Ryan, as he now was, had been appointed Court Secretary in Rabaul. He was subsequently commissioned as a Lieutenant and given regional administration duties. In 1919 Ted left the army but he would have preferred to stay on in New Guinea as a civilian. Health problems from his service in the tropics meant this was not possible and on his return to Melbourne he worked for the Vacuum Oil Company, ultimately in the costing area.

The Ryan family home in Glen Iris was a gallery of photographs—many taken by Ted—as well as objects and artefacts from 'the islands', just like the future homes of his son in country Victoria and in Melbourne. From his father Peter learned the basics of Pidgin English (*Tok Pisin*), a grounding that would prove extremely useful to him within a few years. Ted also gave his son a copy of *Gold Dust and Ashes* by Ion Idriess, sub-titled *The romantic story of the New Guinea goldfields.* Idriess (1889–1979) was an influential and popular Australian author at the time. He wrote more than 50 books on a wide range of historical topics as well as notable bush yarns and outback stories. It was this thoughtful gift from father to son which later on, the recipient said, 'started a passion for New Guinea which 70 years later (this was the 1990s) has not slackened'. As Ryan saw it, that book had 'bent the early twig' of his life.

The older Ryan was remarkably prescient about Japanese intentions in the South West Pacific but did not live to see how they played out. He often discussed his fears with Peter. Oddly enough the two of them would live through some similar war-time experiences, the father in World War One, the son in the World War to come. Their overseas service was in Papua and New Guinea and both would come home with an abiding interest in that area and its people. They were both non-commissioned officers who were promoted to officer rank.

The close bond between the two of them was severed in 1937 when Ted died of cancer, aged 51. Peter was only 13 and felt the loss keenly. It affected him for the rest of his own (much longer) life and he would often speak of the man he had admired and loved. Doreen Ryan returned to work, as a typist, to support her three boys. It had been a devastating blow but fortunately Doreen and her sons had been able to stay in the family home.

Glen Iris is about eleven kilometres east of the Melbourne CBD and was one of the few early suburbs of the city where settlement did not centre on a hotel (or hotels). The first community buildings were a Wesleyan chapel and a school. Residents who arrived in the 1920s recalled open paddocks, unmade roads and mud tracks in winter. Later in his life, long after he left home, Peter Ryan spoke warmly of his formative years in Glen Iris. As he remembered them they had been marked by 'all the advantages of the lower middle class where parents tried bloody hard to get a good education for their kids … all the advantages that they got by economy and sobriety …' It had been a practical upbringing, he said. 'You did not hold ideas beyond your station but you learned that it was possible to rise through prudence, being economical and working hard.'

These were, of course, the closing years of the Depression that would end with the outbreak of war in Europe. Certainly there was no spare money in the Ryan household and even less after the death of Ted. It was two scholarships, not family funds, which enabled his son to attend Malvern Church of England Grammar School (MGS). Peter Ryan's entire schooling, 1928 to 1939, was undertaken at this Anglican school for boys which had opened in 1890. He won the Allen Bequest Scholarship, an open competition for boys in Victoria, and was also awarded a half-scholarship by the school. (In 1947 MGS became Malvern Memorial Grammar School, MMGS, to honour past pupils—like the scholarship boy from Glen Iris—who had fought in the two World Wars. In 1961 it affiliated with Caulfield Grammar School, itself founded in the 1880s.)

A surviving record of the 1930s, copies of the *Malvern Grammarian* magazine, offers a glimpse of Peter Ryan's schooldays. It seems he did play *some* sport (it was probably compulsory) and in his last year was actually in the First XVIII football team as well taking part in house swimming events at the school. Ryan became a strong swimmer, an ability that would prove vital before he was out of his teens. He appears to have had a talent for the Egg & Spoon Race, taking out this challenging event on a number of occasions at school sports days.

But the best indications of the man to come can be found in the magazine's brief details of his literary and drama successes. Year after year his poems and stories were published—a poem 'All Fool's Day' (July 1936) and an article 'Political Impressions' (July 1938), for example. This must have been his first venture into what would be a lifetime of political commentary. (One of his poems is published again in an appendix of this volume along with 'My Tallest Adventure', written when he was 15 years old, not long before what would really be his 'tallest adventure'.) In 1936 he won the open prize for magazine verse and, two years later, for magazine prose. In his last year at MGS he was on the editorial committee of *The Malvern Grammarian.*

Ryan was also an active member of the school Dramatic Society and remembered for the role of a female character in a three-act farce *The Mummy and the Mumps* performed in 1938, and repeated by popular demand the following year. The school magazine reported: 'Peter Ryan, who played the part of Agatha Laidlaw, made an excellent headmistress, supplying just the right amount of pomp and dignity of one who kept her pupils under strict discipline.'

Architect and writer Robin Boyd was a couple of years ahead of him at Malvern Grammar and the athlete John Landy spent his early school days there. In his own class Ryan at one stage shared a two-seater desk with Frank Hughes, another scholarship boy who would go far. Writing about the school near the end of his life the adult Peter Ryan thought it was probably the *humblest* of similar Anglican foundations in the Melbourne of his childhood. 'With an enrolment never much above 200, it was an educational battler,' he wrote in *Quadrant.* It had offered a real-life allegory of *The Vanity of Human Wishes* and a demonstration of *sic transit gloria mundi.* MGS occupied a mansion, now classified by the National Trust of Victoria, in Willoby Avenue, East Malvern. In the twenty-first century it is at the heart of the Malvern campus of Caulfield Grammar School. But when Ryan was there, MGS had no library, one tennis court and a modest 'laboratory' for science studies. Because of its size it was a school where every boy knew every other boy. 'I was happy there,' Ryan said.

Whatever its limitations, long after Ryan and Hughes left Malvern Grammar in 1939 he reckoned they took with them 'the lifetime advantage of having been taught English and History by that paragon of schoolmasters, Gordon "Cactus" Connell'. Ryan thought Connell was a teacher of genius and years later recalled: 'He also infected me with (no one has ever put it better than Gibbon) that early and invincible love of reading which I would not exchange for the treasure of India.'

Connell, in turn, had a high opinion of Ryan, providing him with a glowing testimonial speaking of his character, personality and initiative. For his age, he wrote, 'Peter has excellent educational qualifications. He obtained Leaving Matriculation (in December 1939) passing in English,

French, History, Economics, Geography and Commercial Principles.' (Ryan's School Leaving Certificate shows that he later passed Latin.) Connell added: 'I have taught Peter for five years and have found him outstanding in his general interests. He has a marked gift for literary expression.'

Nor would a reference from Victoria's Minister of Labour, E.J. Mackrell, have harmed the schoolboy's prospects. 'I have known Peter Ryan practically all his life,' he wrote. 'He is a highly intelligent, fine type of young man and is honest and reliable.' All these years later the Mackrell–Ryan connection is not clear. But Edwin Joseph Mackrell was a significant figure in Victorian state politics and had an unusual back story: he had once owned and managed butter factories in South Africa.

When the time came to leave Malvern Grammar, getting a job—any job—presented a formidable challenge for Ryan and Hughes, both well qualified and motivated. The worst of the Depression that began with the Wall Street crash of 1929 was over. But the 1930s in Australia had been a time of high unemployment and poverty which would not end until World War Two. Hughes was employed by an insurance company. Ryan's first job was a junior clerk position in the Commonwealth Railways Melbourne office. When he left after four months the Secretary (T.H. Moyes) noted: 'Master Ryan displayed diligence in the performance of the duties allotted to him and his conduct was entirely satisfactory.' Ryan had resigned to join the Victorian Public

Service as a clerk in the Crown Law Department. The new position was a step closer to his ambition to become a lawyer. He was assigned to the staff of the Master in Equity, Law Courts, Melbourne.

Within a few years Ryan and Hughes would be decorated war heroes: Ryan for covert operations in New Guinea; Hughes for gallantry in the air over Europe. Both would subsequently attend the University of Melbourne and in time Hughes would be a distinguished geologist and leader of the CRA exploration team that discovered Mt Tom Price in Western Australia in 1962.

The schoolboy Ryan's lack of passion for sport did not mean he spent all his leisure time indoors with a good book. In fact some of the skills he developed outdoors would be critically useful much earlier than he could have imagined. As a boy scout and as a lone bushwalker on occasional weekends he built up stamina, learned how to read a map and use a compass. Some of his 'hard bushwalking' experiences he would later describe as foolhardy. Notwithstanding poor eyesight he began to develop 'an eye for country'. This was a term he used in two senses: first the physical challenges, the steepness of terrain, the presence of gullies and so on—in short, how the land might be best traversed; and second the suitability of it for a particular purpose, such as grazing. As a schoolboy Ryan had discovered that minding horses for a local riding school was a congenial way of earning pocket money. He was soon a very good rider himself and after the war he started keeping horses whenever and wherever he could. Reading, riding and walking, he found, were 'activities which combine well with observation and reflection'.

Australians rushed recruitment centres after World War Two broke out in Europe in September 1939. The Royal Australian Navy (RAN) would accept suitable 17-year-olds while the minimum age for the Army (the Militia) and the Royal Australian Air Force (RAAF) was 18. In the early years of the war volunteers to serve abroad with the 2nd AIF had to be 21 years old.

On 10 October 1941, a few weeks after his eighteenth birthday, Ryan joined the Militia. Who knows what his motives were? Australia was not directly threatened at that stage of the war but, as Ted had warned him, the Japanese had their sights on a vast swathe of the Pacific region. Mates would have been joining up and of course there was the prospect of adventure and service. His pride in his late father's role in an earlier conflict would have played a part as well. In one respect at least it cannot have been an easy decision: he would be leaving a happy home, his widowed mother and two brothers still at school.

The new recruit was surprised, yet relieved, that his poor eyesight was not picked up in his medical examination. After basic training at Maribyrnong his group of recruits, many from the Glen Iris area, was assigned to the Royal Australian Engineers (RAE) and sent to 53 Anti-Aircraft

Company (Searchlights). Its strength by then was five officers and more than 300 soldiers and non-commissioned ranks. From here the newcomers were posted to individual 'lights' as they were termed, scattered around Melbourne. Later in the war the Fortress and Anti-Aircraft branches of the RAE would be transferred to the Royal Australian Artillery. But for now, in army nomenclature, he would be Sapper Ryan, of the Engineers. By the time he might have become Gunner Ryan in the Artillery, he was, remarkably, a warrant officer and undertaking secret intelligence work.

When he learned that a similar unit to his own would soon be on its way to Papua, then an Australian Territory, Ryan 'wangled' (his word) a transfer. On 2 March 1942 members of 67 Anti-Aircraft Company sailed from Brisbane for Port Moresby aboard the MV *Macdhui.* Sapper Peter Allen Ryan—army number V144064—was one of them. The *Macdhui* was a three-deck cargo and passenger vessel operated by Burns, Philp & Company of Sydney. It took a week to get to Port Moresby with brief calls at Townsville and Cairns on the way.

You would never guess from a long shipboard letter written to his mother that Sapper Ryan was off to war. Its nine pages made the voyage north sound like a tropical cruise; quite a luxurious one in fact. There were seven-course dinners for a start. The menus posed no problem for the 18-year-old with a school leaving certificate that fortunately included French. Not so some of his mates who looked to him for guidance, particularly on the question of dessert selection.

There had been a dance on board while the *Macdhui* was alongside in Townsville and later the traveller had been very taken with the mountains and islands they passed on the way to Cairns. 'I seem to recall Cactus (Connell) saying all this country consists of drowned volcanoes,' he wrote. 'We are certainly seeing Australia in the de luxe style.' There was also time for reading. Peter was enjoying a book his mother had given him before he left—*Further Experiences of an Irish R.M.* (as in Resident Magistrate).

There was one mention in the letter of preparations for daily life in Papua. Ryan and his mates had attended a lecture on keeping healthy in hot climates. 'It appears that I did the right thing in getting some Johnson's Baby Powder and a tin of Saline before leaving Brisbane.' Very soon he would need a lot more than that.

2
COURAGE AND BETRAYAL

Terrors shall make him afraid on every side, and shall drive him to his feet.

The Book of Job 18.11

Sapper Ryan's war started the day he arrived in Papua. Ten high-flying Japanese aircraft bombed Port Moresby on 9 March 1942, the same day as the men of 67 Anti-Aircraft Company disembarked from the *Macdhui*. No damage was reported from the bombing. The new arrivals would have plenty of work ahead of them as the enemy stepped up its air attacks. Just the day before Japanese forces had landed at Lae and Salamaua on New Guinea's north coast.

Settling in proved easy enough. Ryan's unit was in a Royal Australian Engineers camp on the edge of Port Moresby. Ryan shared a tent with four other men and his first letter home reported satisfaction with the food—mostly tinned but plenty of variety. There was even a refrigerator, a strange sight in the middle of the bush, he thought. As for the air raids, he told the family back in Glen Iris: 'One is merely an interested spectator. When you read newspaper reports of bombing, discount them by about 90 per cent.'

The Japanese had flown their first reconnaissance missions over Port Moresby at the end of January and flying boats bombed the town a few days later. Two months after Ryan's arrival there had been a total of 50 air raids on Port Moresby. His work (searchlights) was at night and as most of the attacks were by day he was soon complaining of boredom. In those early months his unit suffered no casualties.

It was the end of March before Ryan received his first and welcome batch of mail from home since he left Australia. In reply he had a suggestion for the family: how about numbering their letters in the order they were written and posted? His main news was that he had been visiting local villages. The people were quite friendly, he had found. Their neatly fenced and cultivated gardens were a treat to look at with areas of corn, pumpkins, cucumbers, watermelons, pawpaws and bananas.

Three months after his arrival the *Macdhui* incident interrupted the monotony of Sapper Ryan's daytime routine: on successive days Japanese bombers hit the ship in Fairfax Harbour off Port Moresby. Members of the Australian 39th Battalion had been unloading aviation fuel the first day it was attacked. Although the captain manoeuvred the

Macdhui inside the confines of the harbour the ship was damaged and ten crew members were killed or injured. The next day the *Macdhui* was attacked again and this time it took a direct hit, rolled over on a coral reef and sank.

From a hilltop nearby, the war cameraman Damien Parer filmed and photographed the second attack. In his spare time Sapper Ryan had befriended Parer (who was also from Melbourne) and was with him when he recorded the end of the *Macdhui*. Ryan would later describe the scene:

> *The breath of falling bombs seemed to sizzle past our ears. I felt no shame in jumping, shaken, into a slit trench. Looking up, all I could see against the sky were Parer's suede desert boots and one leg of his camera tripod out in the open.*
>
> *'They sounded close to me,' I said. 'Didn't you hear them?'*
>
> *'Didn't hear a thing,' he replied. 'But I was working.'*

Parer was eleven years older than Ryan. In 1944 he was killed by Japanese machine-gun fire on the second day of the allied invasion of Peleliu Island. He was reported to have been walking backwards behind a tank to capture the expression in soldiers' eyes as they went into battle. Parer's acclaimed newsreel film *Kokoda Front Line* had earlier alerted Australian audiences to the realities of the conflict on their doorstep. Doreen Ryan and her boys back in Melbourne must have seen examples of his work when newsreels (as they were called) were screened in local cinemas.

Earlier in 1942 the civil administration of both Papua and New Guinea had been replaced by an Australian Army military government and came under the control of the Australian New Guinea Administrative Unit (ANGAU). This brand-new operation was responsible for conducting civilian activities such as the courts, the police and basic government services; it also undertook a wide range of strictly military and operational duties for the army. One of its major roles was organising the conscription of male villagers who would become cargo carriers, crew members for small coastal vessels, labourers on countless projects and (famously) stretcher bearers for sick and wounded troops. For the rest of his life Peter Ryan never tired in the fight to honour and promote Australia's great debt of friendship to the people of Papua New Guinea.

Around the same time as ANGAU was established the Allied Intelligence Bureau (AIB) was set up by Australia, the Americans, the British and the Dutch. Its role, simply, was to obtain information about the enemy and to do this the AIB co-ordinated and controlled the activities of a wide range of organisations and individuals, in New Guinea and elsewhere.

For its basic structure and leadership ANGAU drew on the hardened, experienced patrol officers and district officers of the pre-war years. There were other jobs to be filled and when Sapper Ryan learned that cadet patrol officers were being recruited he applied at once. His prospects would not have been harmed by a chance encounter in Port Moresby with a lawyer (now an army major) he had known in Melbourne. As luck would have it—and Peter Ryan had a great deal of that in his life—the major was on the selection panel for cadet patrol officers shortly afterwards. Four candidates were successful on that occasion and Peter Ryan, 18, was the youngest of them. The unique demands of the appointment that followed would test him to his physical and mental limits.

The induction program for the cadet patrol officers could be described (generously) as rudimentary. It included one day's legal training for these future Magistrates for Native Matters with power to pass the death sentence for certain grave crimes. All four trainees were apparently relieved to learn that such a sentence could not be carried out without the imprimatur, in writing, of the Commander-in-Chief. At this early stage in the war there was no language training available although in due course these new field recruits would be issued roneoed sheets of key pages from a book of *Tok Pisin* (Pidgin English). Ryan said later they had no training in bushcraft, either, and no preparation for dealing with the local population. However, a few days were set aside at a hospital outside Port Moresby for some first aid and medical instruction. With their induction completed the trainees were promoted in anticipation of their forthcoming responsibilities. In a single bound Sapper Ryan advanced to Warrant Officer (Class 2) Ryan and surely the youngest WO2 in the Australian Army. It was 1 August 1942, five weeks short of his 19th birthday.

About 240 kilometres away—to the north-east of Port Moresby—the town of Wau had recently become the headquarters of the Kanga Force, a composite formation of the Australian Army formed in April 1942. This small and nimble group conducted surveillance and harassment of Japanese forces in occupied Lae and Salamaua. Kanga Force included members of the New Guinea Volunteer Rifles (NGVR), men who were planters, miners and government officials in civilian life, as well as a small number of Australian commandos. It was here that Warrant Officer Ryan was posted.

Getting to Wau at that time was a daunting challenge in itself, involving a small steamer, a whaleboat, a dugout canoe and finally some hard mountain walking. Ryan's luck continued from the first days of his journey. As his small steamer left Port Moresby and made its way to the mouth of the Lakekamu River, a similar vessel in the area was attacked by a Japanese submarine which surfaced and sank it by gunfire. The small steamer with Ryan aboard arrived at its destination without incident. On landing Ryan and his party made their way upstream by whaleboat before transferring to a large dugout canoe which was so deep that its passengers, standing up, could only just peer over the gunwale.

(The Japanese never took Wau. Ryan's route there from Port Moresby followed the remarkable supply line the Australians had established; one which culminated in 50-pound packs of stores being transported over treacherous mountain paths on the backs of native carriers. Ryan thought it was probably one of the most extraordinary lines of communication in military history.)

Ryan's first assignment once he got to Wau beggars belief. The teenage soldier (his mates reckoned he looked like a schoolboy) was dispatched to look for Jock McLeod, a lone Australian, a man he didn't know, somewhere 'out there' in an area of roughly 3,000 square miles. McLeod was a tough career patrol officer and from the mountains behind Lae he was spying on the Japanese. At journey's end (if it ever did) Ryan was to place himself under the orders of McLeod, who had two roles: local governing and administration; and watching the activities of the Japanese invaders.

The young searcher had no map, no compass, a damaged rifle, a revolver that was older than he was (it was 30 years old) with ten rounds of ammunition and a week's supplies, two at a stretch. Nor did he have a radio and in the months ahead any snippet of useful information he gathered would have to be sent back to the nearest secure base by native carrier. The return trip could take several days, sometimes longer. McLeod, the man he would be looking for, didn't have a radio either.

Ryan had a perfunctory knowledge of Pidgin, thanks

to his late father, but it seems reasonable to wonder if his superiors back in Wau expected him to survive, let alone succeed. As the mission began his sole companion was a partly trained native police recruit who Ryan found to be keen but emotionally unstable. His name was Achenmeri and he had no local knowledge or contacts either. First they had to cross the Markham, a swiftly flowing river that began in the Finisterre Range and rushed down to the coast at Lae, about 180 kilometres away.

A couple of years later the young Warrant Officer would recall his elation as they strode out towards the crossing: 'When you are eighteen the fact that quite stupid people can play chuck-ha'penny with your life doesn't seem too unjust. This is partly because the thrill of the adventure is more dangerously intoxicating than liquor. You stride down the jungle trail full of confidence, a pioneer, a new David Livingstone; you feel exactly like your favourite hero from the *Boy's Own Paper.*' In the future, however, there would be days when he would feel on the very brink of madness from loneliness and strain. But not this day.

Along the way they dropped in on a camouflaged Australian commando post named after its founder, Bob Griffiths, an old New Guinea hand who built it at the time of the Japanese invasion. All the scattered Australian posts in those early days of the war were named after somebody known in the Territory—this was Bob's, one was Kirkland's and another Mac's. The post commander at Bob's offered to send Kari, a police lance corporal, on the next stage of the search for Jock. Once again Ryan's luck had made an appearance, for Kari was immensely capable and the pair would become close friends. Ryan, who would stay in touch with him after the war, believed Kari's own story was the stuff of epics. Isolated for months, sometimes deep in enemy territory, he had patrolled for intelligence that had been 'gold' to the planners in Port Moresby and down in Australia. Ryan recalled a man 'cool under fire and a deadly shot. He and his kind were at the apex of a great pyramid of support.'

Once across the Markham the party was on the Huon Peninsula. To the east were Japanese troops in large numbers and to the north the Saruwaged mountains, so high you could not see the tops for clouds, Ryan said. Intelligence at the time reckoned the Japanese 'owned' the other side of the Markham, where Ryan and Kari had now arrived. They pressed on, cautiously, from village to village, aided by a friendly bush telegraph network which spread all kinds of information, particularly the movement of strangers.

Ryan finally located Jock McLeod soon after encountering Ian Downs, a legendary Australian coast watcher who had just had a narrow escape from Japanese soldiers hunting him. Downs was a naval officer and like army Lieutenant John (Jock) Stewart McLeod had been in the Territory as a patrol officer since the mid-1930s. Both of them took extraordinary risks in their daily work and both of them survived the war. (McLeod stayed on and would later be an Assistant District Officer, an ADO, in several districts and in Port Moresby. He died in 1984.) After all his own exertions Ryan got to spend about 24 hours with McLeod. Then the younger man was sent back over the Markham for supplies from an Australian post while McLeod took what was left of Ryan's supplies and slipped away on a reconnaissance mission.

With fresh supplies—and this time a hand-drawn map—Ryan returned to the mountains to finally begin his assignment in the Wain country: moving from village to village gathering any information of value while dispensing basic medical (and other) help and advice. Trade goods he carried were helpful in this work, items like razor blades (much sought after), a supply of New Guinea shillings, coarse salt and sheets of newspapers for rolling cigarettes. These were considered passive intelligence activities but there were more active forays to come. From the start Warrant Officer Ryan was living dangerously and every day life-and-death decisions had to be made: What danger might lie just ahead? Which path to follow? Whom to trust when you got there? These were quite apart from such basic issues as food supply, shelter for the night, dealing with fatigue and loneliness; not to mention fevers in the extremes of heat and cold. Even monotony at times.

Over the next 12 months Ryan would be one of a handful of Australian loners out there on the Huon Peninsula with a brief, as he would later put it, 'To keep an eye on the Japs' and at the same time 'Keep in touch with the native situation.' All this in a terrain that ranged from freezing mountains to swampy and malarial river flat-lands. Sometimes, for weeks at a stretch, he would lie down to sleep at night with, as he put it, the lively expectation of being dead by dawn. 'Certainly this frightened me,' he admitted. 'But I had learned by then that tranquillity can be preserved even in the midst of terror: mostly I slept as sweetly as if I had been in bed in my mother's house.'

On one occasion, hunted by Japanese soldiers with tracker dogs, he sought safety by climbing 'a stupendous dry cascade of huge boulders as it ascended ever higher up a mountainside'. As he rested about 10,000 feet up, a school geography lesson drifted into his mind: This chaotic wasteland of rocks was the moraine left behind when an ancient glacier retreated. Exhausted at the high altitude Ryan imagined a booming voice: 'This is the end of the earth. You've reached the end of the earth.' His response had been: If ever I get out of this I'll never travel anywhere again. (While he returned to Papua New Guinea from Australia countless times, he never visited Europe or America, indeed anywhere else outside the South West Pacific.)

When his war was over, one man in particular had helped keep him alive: Singin Pasom, a loyal villager, a *tultul*, an official who exercised government authority in minor local matters. It was in this capacity that the *tultul* first met Ryan, secretly at the junction of two obscure mountain tracks. Lutheran missionaries had been a major influence in his upbringing in a village a couple of days' walk inland from Lae. In his youth, it was said (he was born about 1908) he had been outstanding in vigour and intelligence. For the young Australian who entered his life in 1942 he never failed to deliver on promises of food and carriers through the area and performed many other acts of kindness and service; not the least of these warning when Japanese were approaching.

After the war Papa Singin, as he became known, was a Member of Parliament and a grateful Ryan visited him in Papua New Guinea many times. Ryan talked with Dongau, his hero's daughter-in-law, after the old man died in 1998. Referring to those perilous days of 1942–43, he wondered: 'I must have been an appalling worry to him just then. He had every reason to hate me for being anywhere near his ground. Why was he always so kind?' Dongau had smiled and responded: 'I know the answer to that. He felt sorry for you. You were so young. You should not have been out by yourself.'

As the months of that early New Guinea campaign went by the dangers multiplied for the Australians behind the enemy lines. After learning (but only when it was over) of a hazardous journey Ryan made to the outskirts of occupied Lae the Japanese put a price—dead or alive—on his head: Two cases of meat plus five Australian pounds. It was never collected. Audaciously, Ryan and his small police party had interrogated Chinese prisoners of the Japanese near Lae, then quickly moved on before the alarm was raised.

Later, in the most dramatic incident of his war service, Ryan's luck almost ran out. After a gruelling trek over the mountains with Captain Les Howlett (another experienced Patrol Officer) he arrived in the village of Chivasing which they expected would still be friendly to them. However, local natives had betrayed them and the Japanese lay waiting in ambush. On approaching the centre of the settlement the pair came under heavy fire and Howlett was hit as they made a dash for a nearby creek. He was wounded and subsequently killed.

Ryan struggled across the creek and into the bush having lost his Owen gun and most of his badly ripped shirt. On the other side he buried himself deep in a mud patch where pigs used to wallow, with only his nose showing. He could hear the Japanese calling out to each other and their feet sucking and squelching in the mud as they searched for him. Half an hour later some villagers tried to trick him by calling out that the Japanese had moved on. But of course they hadn't.

When it was nearly dark Ryan climbed out of the mud, wiped the muck off his revolver and compass and began the long, hard walk home.

In a couple of years of bad journeys that first night's travel would be the worst he could remember. Then after swimming the Markham (currents and crocodiles notwithstanding) he travelled downstream aboard a purloined canoe to the relative safety of Kirkland's post. There he was greeted by startled soldiers who helped their tattered and exhausted fellow countryman to shelter and a meal. Soon after, Kari and the rest of Ryan and Howlett's police team arrived, dispirited and tired but pleased to see him. They had stayed behind looking for Ryan after the ambush. Once they found his tracks to the river they concluded he had escaped so they made their own way to Kirkland's, floating themselves on logs. A few days later, unable to walk confidently, Ryan made his way on horseback to Bulolo township, which had replaced Wau as the area military quarters. There—in a scene that could have been out of an Evelyn Waugh novel—he was berated by an army quartermaster for losing his pay book and other papers. Did he not know this was a serious offence?

In February 1944, Tuya, the guide who led the Japanese patrol that ambushed Howlett and Ryan, was executed by the Australian authorities for the murder of the wounded Captain Howlett. Tuya was not from Chivasing and in one of his patrol reports Ryan had noted that he 'had spent the pre-war years in Lae gaol'. Villagers—some 1,300 of them—were brought in from the Markham, the Wain and elsewhere to witness the public hanging. The execution took place above the beach at Tuya's home village, Wagang, near Lae.

Ryan and Howlett's fateful patrol mission had been conducted between 25 April and 23 June 1943. No European had been in the area since Ryan was withdrawn in January that year. The pair were instructed to re-establish contact with, and secure the confidence of, the native population of the Wain and Naba areas, and to gather information on enemy activity in Lae and the Huon Peninsula generally. The patrol included an eight-man native police contingent led by Lance Corporal Kari and was equipped with an ATR4 radio to communicate with Port Moresby.

The 32-page intelligence report filed by Ryan on his return was written from memory. As the Warrant Officer explained at the start of his report: 'The diary kept jointly by Captain Howlett and myself was captured on Howlett's body.' As the report had been written from memory, he continued, there might be slight inaccuracies of time and dates. It was certainly a detailed and engrossing document.

The patrol had found many signs of Japanese visitors to some of the villages they checked—in one case spotting a pile of cigarette butts where a sentry had been posted. Sometimes there were new tracks cut or changes to village structures. It was often difficult terrain to move through—some of it rugged, some jungle, always potentially dangerous. Several times native carriers had attempted to throw down their loads and run away; Kari had always forestalled them. Early in June the patrol was ordered to withdraw from the Huon Peninsula after Harry Lumb, another Australian out there, had been betrayed and then killed by a Japanese patrol. Two weeks later Captain Howlett was killed at Chivasing.

Ryan's report detailed Japanese propaganda activities the patrol learned about. 'The activities of the black mission teachers and the great power they now wield' were the most outstanding feature of the native situation. These teachers, he wrote, were possessed of an anti-European (and particularly anti-government) complex; 'the lengths they will go to to obstruct the way of a patrol is almost unbelievable'. His report ended with a tribute to the police and indentured labourers who had accompanied the patrol.

Ryan's lonely war was coming to an end, though not just yet. Patched up, briefly rested and reclothed, he left Bulolo with a small police detachment to patrol a stretch of the Markham where the Americans were planning to build new airstrips. The push to drive the Japanese out of New Guinea was on in earnest by now and Tex Frazier, an American engineer, joined the patrol group. Ryan liked him, found him frank and engaging, but there was a problem: Nobody knew if there were Japanese in the area or not and Tex liked to burst into song as the patrol made its way (cautiously) through the bush. He found it so hard to stop that Ryan detailed a policeman to walk nearby and silence any outburst before it gave them away.

In September 1943 Ryan's health finally caught up with him—malaria, hookworm, skin problems, general debility—and he was evacuated from the field to an army hospital in Port Moresby. From there in a letter home to his mother—marked *Cleared by Censor*—he reported he was 'cooped up in bed having a course of quinine, atabrine and what not'. He was hoping for some leave once he was well again but warned her that it might take a little time to come through. She should not count on it. A couple of weeks later and shortly after his 20th birthday he was evacuated to Australia by air.

When he arrived in Townsville on 11 October 1943 his various medical conditions meant he was 'pretty crook'. In the measure of those times he weighed just six and a half stone (about 41 kilos) and for the rest of his life he would suffer malaria attacks. After three months of spells in military hospitals and some home leave Warrant Officer Ryan was pronounced fit for limited duties. At this point—late in January 1944—he was about to enjoy yet another remarkable piece of good fortune.

It was triggered by a chance encounter in Melbourne's Collins Street with Nick Penglase, a District Officer he had known and respected in New Guinea. Warrant Officer Ryan had asked Major Penglase (as he now was): 'What are you doing here?' and the major had responded: 'I'm working for a bunch of weirdos at Victoria Barracks.' This was shorthand for the army's strange and exotic Directorate of Research and Civil Affairs (DORCA). After a few drinks the two men went to Victoria Barracks where Ryan was introduced around. One of those he met was Colonel Alfred Conlon who ran the show. A decision Conlon made shortly afterwards to recruit him probably saved his life.

Ryan's immediate difficulty was that the army had another assignment for him: a secret mission with a small team to New Britain, a large island off the New Guinea coast. Ryan thought the project was 'hare-brained' and would fail. (It did, and most of the participants perished.) Nor did he believe he was fit enough for more hard bush work. Conlon, when he heard about it (from Ryan) told the 20-year-old Warrant Officer: 'Go back to the Caulfield Racecourse Leave and Transit Depot and tell whoever is in charge that the Commander-in-Chief requires your body to be produced here at Victoria Barracks at 9.30 in the morning.'

The duty officer at the depot was not impressed and in the absence of written orders it was hardly surprising that Ryan's request was refused. But then, hours before he was to leave for New Guinea, Warrant Officer Ryan was summoned to the depot orderly room. There he was told that a staff car had arrived with written orders for him to proceed at once to Victoria Barracks. And that, Ryan would say later, was Alf Conlon at work.

The Directorate had been set up in April 1942 at Army Headquarters in Melbourne. Most of its officers, including Ryan himself in due course, were directly commissioned via the army's Special List. What a diverse, talented and eccentric collection of men and women they were—among them academics, an anthropologist or two, New Guinea patrol officers, artists, poets, lawyers, a Gallipoli veteran and a veterinarian. Ryan was one of a small number of recruits whose recent active service in the New Guinea region would be of direct relevance to the Directorate's work.

And this was where the young Warrant Officer with a school leaving certificate and an unusual military background began to assemble a network of friends and valuable contacts who would populate parts of his life for decades. Ryan was transferred from the Militia to the AIF and allocated a new army number, VX128541.

It was more than 60 years before much of the myth and mystery of the Directorate of Research and Civil Affairs was stripped away in a closely researched history entitled *The Backroom Boys* (2013). In the words of author Graeme Sligo, a career soldier, the army's Directorate was 'essentially a policy advice bureau for General Blamey'. (Blamey, later Field Marshal Sir Thomas Blamey, was appointed Commander-in-Chief of the Australian Military Forces in 1942 and Commander of allied land forces in the South West Pacific area under the command of US General Douglas MacArthur.)

Conlon himself was (and remains) an intriguing figure: controversial and charming, he seems to have been a genius in recruiting talent and had a voracious appetite for knowledge. Sligo noted that Conlon had the ability to form relationships with powerful people and advise them of intelligent ways of resolving or solving their particular problems. A Sydney University graduate (Arts) he also studied medicine and became a psychiatrist after the war. Major Alf Conlon was 33 on appointment and soon advanced to Lieutenant Colonel and then Colonel. Ryan liked him (well, he did owe him a considerable debt) and wrote at length about him in a volume of 15 profiles entitled *Brief Lives* published in 2004. The essay on Conlon was twice the length of any of the others. At DORCA Ryan's duties included investigating and preparing reports on problems of civil government in occupied territories. Other assignments included a survey of the copra industry and a brief history of Papuan government plantations. It was Conlon who picked up Ryan's eyesight problem and not before time specialist advice was sought. The DORCA chief had noticed the Warrant Officer often suffered severe headaches when he had been doing a lot of close reading.

In the post-war years many of the men and women who passed through the Directorate would play major roles in government, the professions and public life. Conlon's deputy, for example, was John Kerr, Colonel John Kerr by the end of the war and later Governor-General of Australia. Major James Plimsoll was later Secretary of the (then) Department of External Affairs and Governor of Tasmania. John Legge, a lifelong friend of Ryan, was Foundation Professor of History at Monash University, while Major Ida Lesson, an accomplished librarian, would later do Ryan, the writer, a very great service. Other DORCA alumni included Major Harry Gibbs, later Sir Harry Gibbs, Chief

Justice of the High Court of Australia; and Warrant Officer Leslie Bury, a future Federal Treasurer and Minister for Foreign Affairs and for Labour and National Service. The Ern Malley poetry hoax was concocted in 1943 by two uniformed poets in DORCA, Lieutenant James McAuley and Corporal Harold Stewart. Their work—undertaken one weekend at Victoria Barracks—has been described as the greatest literary hoax of the 20th century. McAuley, later Professor of English at the University of Tasmania, was also the founding editor of *Quadrant* which published a monthly column by Peter Ryan from 1994 until his death in 2015. Author Graeme Sligo concluded his study of the organisation: 'Largely unknown today, Alfred Conlon and his backroom boys bequeathed a substantial legacy to post-war Australia.'

On 25 April 1944 Melbourne's *Argus* reported that Warrant Officer Ryan had been awarded the Military Medal. (The citation read: 'Outstanding courage and devotion—Markham 25/4/43'.) The newly decorated soldier thought his superiors had known of the award for some time before he did; hardly surprising, if true, given the Directorate's connections. The MM was an award to British and Commonwealth personnel below commissioned rank for bravery in battle on land. The recommendation for Ryan's personal award was made by General Blamey and Lieutenant General E.F. (Ned) Herring, GOC New Guinea Force.

Their advice to the British War office read:

> *On 25 April 1943 W.O.2 Ryan accompanied Capt. Howlett (FELO) on an intelligence and propaganda patrol of the Huon Peninsula area in the Markham district—a task of most hazardous nature while operating in almost impenetrable jungle and bleak mountainous country, surrounded by enemy and hostile natives.*
>
> *On 9 June the patrol, acting under instructions, withdrew and on 21 June was ambushed at Chivasing by a strong Japanese force assisted by natives. Here the officer in charge, Capt. Howlett, was killed.*
>
> *Only by excellent bushcraft, endurance and coolness was W.O. Ryan able to make his escape and report back to his base with intelligence of great importance. During the final episode W.O. Ryan swam the Markham River, in itself a feat of magnitude.*
>
> *It is considered the courage and devotion to duty displayed by W.O. Ryan, on this and previous occasions, most meritorious and deserving of immediate recognition.*

Ryan and other recipients of awards for service in the South West Pacific were later presented with their medals by the Governor-General, the Duke of Gloucester, at Government House in Melbourne. In March 1945 Warrant

Officer Ryan was awarded another decoration—Mentioned In Dispatches with Oak Leaf Insignia and the citation Distinguished Service in S.W. Pacific. (An MID recipient is a soldier whose name appears in an officer's report to a superior officer which is passed on to high command. It describes gallant or meritorious service in the face of the enemy and is a prized decoration. Ryan was entitled to other service medals when World War Two ended: the 1939–45 Star, the Pacific Star and the Australian Service Medal.)

Two weeks after his MID was gazetted Warrant Officer Ryan was commissioned as a Lieutenant (Special List) and appointed as an Instructor at the army's new Land Headquarters School of Civil Affairs in the Australian Capital Territory.

The school, established late in 1944 in the grounds of the Royal Military College, Duntroon, has been described as a remarkable educational experiment. It was under the control of the army's Director of Research (Colonel Conlon extending his influence) and was tasked with training staff for the administrative service of Australian New Guinea. The idea, initially, was to run short courses of about four months' duration for groups of servicemen. Graduates would be commissioned and most sent north as patrol officers. After the war they would be encouraged to stay on in the civilian administration. In 1946 the school morphed into the Australian School of Pacific Administration and DORCA's John Kerr was appointed its first civilian principal.

As an instructor at the school, Ryan was well equipped to teach his students Pidgin and introduce them to many practical matters they might soon face as patrol officers. The Lieutenant would willingly admit it was a 'soft' job. And just as well it was as he had other things on his mind: a girl he would later marry and a book he was writing.

Ryan liked to claim that the girl had picked him up while he was on leave back in Glen Iris. It seems more likely that they met at a tram stop where he was engrossed in a book. Whatever the explanation Ryan had seen enough to find out where she was staying and to call on her, bearing flowers, soon after. Her real name was Gladys Davidson, but since her school days she has been universally known as Davey. Miss Davidson was 19 and a comptometer operator. She had a boyfriend but Ryan saw him off. Davey was the daughter of a farmer and pub owner at Tambo Crossing in East Gippsland. More than 50 years later Peter Ryan admitted: 'I thought that was marvellous. I was going to marry the daughter of a grazier who owned a pub. But the pub got burnt down and wool prices slumped so there was no percentage in that. But I got a sterling wife out of it.'

'Cactus' Connell, the Malvern Grammar English and History teacher Ryan admired so much, now proved helpful to him once more. Lieutenant Ryan had an idea for a book and recalled Connell's advice not even to start writing unless there was something to say; and if there was, to say it simply. Yes, there was, he decided; and yes, he would. Much that was of interest had happened to him in 1942–43 but where to start the story? What to leave out? In the end he decided to focus his writing on a series of intelligence patrols in the general region of New Guinea's Markham River. Then he set to work, writing by hand and 'in the quiet nights of Canberra a small and rather nervous manuscript built up'. Over the next few years several publishers would have a look at *Fear Drive My Feet*. But the writer would have to wait until 1959 to see his manuscript in book form and welcomed with great acclaim.

The Pacific War ended on 2 September 1945 and Lieutenant Ryan was demobilised just over two months later, on 13 November. His army papers recorded 752 days active service in Australia and 589 days overseas. Sapper, Warrant Officer and Lieutenant, he had been tested (and had flourished) in extraordinary conditions and proved to be courageous in the field; and now, at 22, he was a junior member of a diverse and influential network. His card had been marked: a young man of promise.

The next few months would be a time of peace, if not quiet. The experienced bushwalker found work in a sawmill in the middle of nowhere, outside the Victorian country town of Warburton. This was at Starling's Gap, one of the surviving isolated communities which had been part of Victoria's premier sawmilling district. It was an area he had explored before he went to war; a good place to recuperate before starting university studies in a few months' time.

3

WINDING ROAD AHEAD

No bar or dinner table failed to buzz with expectant pleasure when Cyril Pearl approached.

Peter Ryan

There was only one university in Victoria in 1946 and its single campus was seriously overcrowded with the influx of ex-servicemen. Some of them were still in uniform. In his first few days at the University of Melbourne that year Peter Ryan, demobilised soldier, met Able Seaman Creighton Burns, still in the Royal Australian Navy but not in uniform. The two would be close and supportive mates for the next 60 years.

The term *golden age* has often been used to describe those early post-war years at Melbourne University. At least a third of the students were ex-servicemen with what Ryan would later describe as a shrewd knowledge of the world and a passionate desire to retrieve the lost years of their lives. He had enrolled under the auspices of the Commonwealth

Reconstruction Training Scheme which paid his university fees and a modest personal allowance (by 1951 more than 300,000 ex servicemen and women had signed up for education and vocational training courses under this scheme). Three years later he graduated BA (Hons) after majoring in History and taking some subjects in Law, Logic, English and French. Many of his contemporaries would rise to the top of their professions: Edward (later Sir Edward) Woodward would one day be Chancellor of the University and Austin Asche, Chief Justice and subsequently Administrator of the Northern Territory. Creighton Burns edited the *Age* and was later the inaugural Chancellor of the Victoria University of Technology. Ryan himself would become an essayist of note and—for 26 years—Director of Melbourne University Press.

After the war ended there were growing fears, world-wide, about the threat of Communism and in 1945 a major report by the Australian Security Service warned of the danger posed by the Communist Party of Australia. Information gathered on individuals at that time—some of it amateurish, some of it plain wrong—reflected these concerns. The historian and author Geoffrey Blainey wrote of his friend Peter Ryan that like most ex-servicemen at the end of the war his politics veered more to the Left. With his intelligence background and DORCA experience Ryan was promising fodder for the security authorities. From his early student days they took an interest in him.

Between 1946 and 1948 he was secretary and then

president of the University Labour Club and without offering any compelling detail informants reported Ryan was 'extremely left wing'. Despite its suspicions—which lingered well beyond the target's student days—the security service recorded not only Ryan's denial that he was a Communist; but also the fact that he was apparently *persona non grata* with members of the party branch at the University. At one point the security service formed the view that while not a Communist Party member Ryan was fairly close to the party. The file noted he 'would probably move away from it'. They certainly got that bit right. Ryan helped see off Communist Party attempts to take over the University Labour Club and gradually became more conservative himself. Much later, in 1997, he reflected on the pervasive power of the Communist Party in his student days, even claiming that from the background the Communists had virtually controlled the Labour Club.

There was a flicker of concern when Ryan stood as an independent candidate (unsuccessfully) for the safe Liberal seat of Toorak in the Victorian election of 1947. Posters appeared throughout the electorate during the campaign warning that RYAN SPELLS RUIN. His security dossier, quoting the political journal *News Weekly*, queried why a man whose political tastes lean to militant Marxism was a candidate at all. (In 1949 domestic security became the responsibility of the new Australian Security Intelligence Organisation, ASIO. In 1954—after a review by the

Director General—Ryan's file was updated to state that he 'no longer presents a security risk'.)

As far as his studies were concerned it was various history subjects that occupied most of his time. When Ryan was an undergraduate Professor Max Crawford was the driving force in the History Department at the University of Melbourne. Through its talented graduates the department was recognised at the time as having a profound influence on the teaching of history in Australian universities and schools. Ryan and Creighton Burns never forgot their first history lecture which was delivered to a crowded lecture theatre in the Zoology building. Ryan was still talking about the occasion 60 years later. The subject was British History B and on that day, he recalled, 'It wasn't a lecturer mounting a podium. It was a performer mounting the stage.' This was Kathleen Fitzpatrick, senior lecturer in history, inspired and inspiring teacher, a striking, theatrical and beautifully groomed woman. Two years later this Oxford graduate and author was elevated to Associate Professor, only the third woman at the University to achieve that rank; and the first in Australia outside the natural sciences.

In his second year at the University Ryan encountered Manning Clark, recruited by Crawford to establish the first full-scale course in Australian history. More than any other, Ryan would later admit, Manning Clark had made the study of Australian history interesting; a discipline in its own right. The two were soon firm friends and Ryan would later publish five of the six volumes of Clark's ground-breaking *History of Australia.* Then—in 1993 when Clark had been dead for more than two years—Ryan would unleash an extraordinary attack on his former lecturer's work, his reputation and his character. There would be a lot of drinking, partying and publishing before that day came. 'I always found his company agreeable because he was amusing and well read,' Ryan would later tell an interviewer. 'It was never hard to find topics of conversation.'

Nobody Ryan met at University made a greater impression on him than William Macmahon Ball. 'Mac', as he was universally known, has been described as a towering figure in the intellectual and public life of 20th-century Australia. In 1949, after Ryan had graduated, the University of Melbourne created its first chair of political science. Mac Ball was appointed and filled the role with distinction for 19 years. In a charming and attractive little memoir published after Mac's death in 1986 Ryan wrote of a man 'whose life was anything but academic in the narrow sense. He was a splendid journalist, an avid though not extravagant punter on the horses, one of Australia's most esteemed radio speakers, author of books, dropper-in to the pub with locals, teacher within the University and outside and an Australian diplomat.' The Ryan family often visited the Macmahon Balls in Eltham and the two men continued to lunch regularly after Mac retired.

Ryan was still at University when he and Davey were

married on 23 May 1947 in St John's Anglican Church, Finch Street, Malvern East. The ceremony was conducted by an uncle of the bride. Ryan was not a churchgoer himself but he certainly had wide ecumenical associations. When he was 13 he had won a Scripture Prize at school. Ted Ryan was what used to be referred to as 'a lapsed Catholic', and his son said the Ryan family used to trot off happily to the Methodist church about half a dozen times a year. The young Peter attended an Anglican grammar school, partly on a Presbyterian Church administered scholarship and on joining the army declared his religion as Presbyterian. Once his army training began he found it convenient to line up on church parade with the Catholic recruits. This involved a welcome Sunday morning trip outside the camp to a parish church followed by a couple of quick beers at an accommodating pub on the way back. Looking back on those days much later he would say that a couple of years' active war service persuaded him to respect any man's sincere religious belief, 'so long as he would indulge me in my doubt'. Irrespective of the 'truth' of the Christian revelation he was convinced Christianity was still the most wholesome doctrine of ethical regulation the world had so far evolved.

Mr and Mrs Peter Ryan began their married life in a large room on the top floor of an old rooming house in Flinders Street, overlooking the Jolimont railway yards. In some respects it would not be a conventional union but their long and happy marriage ended only with Peter's death 68 years later. Ryan's position in the Victorian Public Service had been kept open for him while he was in the army but he had resigned to study full time at University. At the end of 1947 he had sought a reference from his former employer and in one of those *To whom it may concern* statements one of his former supervisors advised: 'I formed a very high opinion of his efficiency, initiative and integrity.'

Unlike his friend Burns (who was the Victorian Rhodes Scholar in 1949) Ryan did not go down the academic path after leaving university. Nor does he seem to have considered schoolteaching. Certainly he would have been well suited to daily journalism but graduates were not recruited in significant numbers until the 1960s, newspapers preferring to hire their cadets (as they were called) straight from school. Instead he began his post-war civilian career publishing, as he would put it, 'comics and other rubbish'. In fact Ryan would play a small part in the development of the comic book in Australia. Over the next 14 years—before he settled down, you might say—he also tried advertising, the emerging field of public relations and came to notice as a gifted freelance writer. There were also brief periods of unemployment.

Ryan's entry to the world of 'comics and other rubbish' had actually been made while he was still at university. Soon after it was established in 1947 he had been offered a position with a new business, Atlas Publications, and before long was appointed manager. Not that he had any qualifications or background in management. This would be just one of several jobs he would have in his life where he would start off *cold.* His new employer had offices above a furniture warehouse in the inner Melbourne suburb of Clifton Hill. It had been set up by a fascinating trio of veteran newspapermen: Jack Bellew, George Warnecke and Clive Turnbull. Ryan would later describe them as a small syndicate of well-off Melbourne lefty journalists. J.W. (Jack) Bellew (1901–57), educated at Scotch College and the University of Melbourne, had been a newspaper executive and was part of the Heide circle of John and Sunday Reed. G.W. (George) Warnecke (1894–81) had worked in journalism in Australia, Britain and the USA. He had conceived, designed and delivered the idea of the *Australian Women's Weekly* and was its first editor when it appeared in 1933. S.C. (Clive) Turnbull (1906–75), a respected writer, author and poet, has been described as the 'doyen' of Melbourne's journalist community. Atlas took off with the *Captain Atom* comic produced by two Australians: the gifted illustrator and writer Arthur Mather, and Bellew himself, writing under the name John Welles. *Captain Atom* was created to celebrate the atomic age and was an immediate hit, selling one million copies in 1948. (*Captain Atom* was one newspaper critic's favourite character at a State Library of Victoria exhibition of Australian comics in 2006. She described 'a wooden looking jut-jawed fellow in a red costume, a yellow helmet and a belt that appears to deflect bullets'.

The business quickly expanded with a list of locally produced and imported comic books, magazines and joke books. There were also cheap western novelettes—*Gunshot Westerns.* At one point Ryan was writing one of these a month, sometimes two. Years later he would explain that first he had needed to master a minimal vocabulary; something like 'Why you ornery, low down, side-winding coyote, a man oughta pistol whip you.' But his day job, of course, was managing Atlas, a challenging role in a growing business that none of the principals were really that proud of. Yet it presented a rare opportunity for Ryan to gain valuable hands-on production and management experience, given that he had none to begin with. From his mid-20s he was responsible for publishing, printing, merchandising, administration and distribution. Ryan was also introduced to advisory and publication work in the public relations field when his duties were broadened to include Atlas Associates, a business concerned exclusively with PR.

Clive Turnbull—something of a man-about-town by this time—soon recognised Ryan's great capacity for friendship and camaraderie. As the journalist Robert Murray pointed out it was Turnbull who introduced the younger man to the 'chummy ranks of the intelligentsia and sometime Bohemia'. What a happy milieu it would be for the engaging young man who came to it—alert and interested—with a unique story of his own. One of his new circle, Cyril Pearl (1904–87), became a cherished friend and dining companion. Ryan once said generously of him: 'No bar or dinner table failed to buzz with expectant pleasure when Cyril Pearl approached.' Pearl (author of *Wild Men of Sydney*) also provided an uncanny role model: 'Journalist, author, historian, mischief merchant and provocateur, scourge of the pompous, scholar, wit, bon-vivant, gentleman and man of courage.' This was Ryan's description of someone he admired enormously, whose company he sought out. Long after the death of both of them we now know it could equally apply to the younger man. (With a few additions such as: can be dogmatic, not to be crossed, cantankerous at times.)

The Ryan family had grown to three in 1951 with the arrival of Andrew and they moved into a large old house called Dalkeith at 223 Burke Road, Glen Iris. It was occupied by maiden aunts of Peter who divided the house in two to accommodate the newcomers. Davey, Peter and Andrew lived at Dalkeith for ten years and were joined by Andrew's sister Sally in 1958. With his growing responsibilities Ryan started looking around with a view to improving his longer-term prospects. He applied (unsuccessfully) for a number of jobs including a position as a Trade Commissioner, at that time (1952) in the Federal Department of Commerce and Agriculture. It is not clear what happened in this instance but he didn't get the job and ASIO delayed consideration of his application. By July 1953 he had resigned from Atlas and was briefly unemployed. Whatever the 'serious personal disagreement' was with his managing director he left with a glowing reference from Jack Bellew praising the 'very large part' he had played in the expansion of Atlas Publications. Bellew underlined one particular trait of his departing manager: 'His personality speaks for itself,' he wrote. 'One of his greatest assets has been his ability to make friends for the company wherever he has made contacts.' For Ryan (and particularly Davey) this was a worrying time with no income, rent to be paid to the aunts and a small boy to be cared for. Then the advertising industry beckoned.

When he joined United Service Publicity it was the largest advertising agency in Melbourne and well regarded overseas. It had been set up by the businessman Alfred (later Sir Alfred) Kemsley, known as Kem, who had been Director of Organisation and Recruiting at Army Headquarters in Melbourne during the war. Ryan was hired as personal assistant to the managing director. A few weeks later he was appointed production manager with responsibility for all mechanical production of press material and printed matter. He was subsequently a partner in the business (which became USP Benson in 1962) and an associate director.

One of Andrew Ryan's earliest memories has a USP connection. When he was four, maybe five, the Ryan family looked after a boy named Robert Wilson during the school holidays. His parents were on a six-month overseas trip and his father, Harper Wilson, was a USP director. The house guest took the small boy to the local newsagents and bought him a Donald Duck comic. Peter Ryan (who knew a bit about comics) picked it up, thought it was great, and from that day the Duck family was part of the Ryan family. More than 60 years later Andrew Ryan still has two boxes of Donald Duck comics, the remains of the family collection. His father's view was that anything that encouraged reading was a good thing. 'A lot of my friends weren't allowed comics,' Andrew recalls. 'So the Ryan house was a great place to visit.'

On 4 July 1957 the USP newsletter recorded that with extreme regret the board had accepted the resignation of Peter Ryan. He was leaving the agency, it said, to take a most important executive post with Imperial Chemical Industries. Two months earlier Ryan had applied to the executive selection business of John P. Young & Associates in response to newspaper advertisements for a Public Relations Officer. The company was identified only as 'An Australia-wide manufacturing organisation'. It was seeking a man (*sic*) with a wide knowledge of Australian industrial and commercial practice and preferably journalistic and publishing experience. The successful candidate would have to be capable of handling public relations activities at a high level.

Ryan was offered the position on 28 June 1957 with Imperial Chemical Industries of Australia and New Zealand Limited (ICIANZ). His prospects were certainly looking up. Public relations as a management activity was in its infancy in Australia and the company had a big task for him. His salary at 3,000 pounds a year plus benefits was generous. In his resignation letter to Kemsley, Ryan explained that the ICI offer was 'in all respects so remarkably attractive that I have really no practical alternative but to accept it'. His parting gift to Kem was a warmly received copy of a *Dictionary of Quotations*.

Imperial Chemical Industries of Australia and New Zealand was a Melbourne based, UK owned manufacturing company producing paints, fertilisers and explosives. It also had a large fabrics business. Long after Ryan had gone it changed its name to Imperial Chemical Industries (ICI) and in 1998 it became Orica Limited.

The company's new Public Relations Officer—soon to be elevated to Public Relations Manager—had arrived just in time to prepare for a major PR opportunity at ICIANZ. This was the opening of ICI House, its striking new headquarters in East Melbourne. On completion the next year (1958) it would be the tallest building in Australia and the first international-style skyscraper in the country. ICI House caused great excitement, attracting enormous corporate, professional and public interest. An estimated 20,000 people inspected the building during an Open Week organised by Ryan's public relations department. They toured a remarkable edifice that was different to anything the city had seen before. ICI House was clad in glass curtain walls to the north and south while inside features included an early open plan design, a ground floor theatre and a 400-

seat staff cafeteria with stunning 360-degree views. The mass circulation *Herald* (it was selling more than 435,000 copies a day at the time) was very impressed. It suggested that probably no other Melbourne building project since the Exhibition Building in the 1870s had created such a stir as this glass-house giant.

Peter Ryan thought the new building and the fuss surrounding its appearance were an 'unimaginable boon' for the company. For a time, he said, editors and journalists from around Australia would do almost anything to be invited on a personal tour, followed by lunch in one of the private dining rooms. In the midst of all this excitement Ryan prepared the way for Geoffrey Blainey to be invited to write a history of the company. The pair didn't know each other well at this point but the Ryan and the Blainey families would become good friends. The two men had met in the mid-1950s at a supper party and Blainey also remembered the first time he saw the name Peter Ryan; it was on an election poster (that would be 1947) attached to a lamp post near Melbourne's Wesley College. Blainey was just completing a history of the National Bank of Australasia and was given space in ICI House for his new project. It was delivered on time but the company, for its own corporate reasons, decided against publication.

Two years after it was opened, ICI House, its owners and its public relations department faced a major problem. Glass panes from the iconic building began to shatter and fall, more than 70 of them eventually. Timber canopies were quickly erected to protect passers-by below. The fortnightly journal *Nation* was on to the story courtesy of its 'Melbourne Spy'. The *Nation* columnist drew attention to problems with some post-war buildings in Australia. Enough chunks and fragments were falling from buildings to make a stroll around Melbourne 'a more adventurous excursion than a quiet citizen might realise'.

The column, which was sub-titled 'Chips off the New Glass Blocks', continued:

> *The most celebrated case is that of the towering ICI building, the city's tallest. Designed by the leading architectural firm of Bates, Smart and McCutcheon, it is said to have cost three million pounds. It was once whimsically described by the witty architect-writer Robin Boyd as Melbourne's elegant top hat—a description whose aptness one can appreciate, even without being certain whether such a metaphor implies praise for the building's undoubted elegance, or gentle admonition of its impending archaism.*
>
> *The building seems recently to have developed snakelike tendencies, an inclination to shed its skin. Regrettably for passing pedestrians, the skin is made of glass, and so Nicholson Street is sometimes thickly showered with shining vitreous particles which may have fallen from a height of anything up to 250 feet. Melbourne's top hat has*

therefore acquired a somewhat adventitious new stiff brim, in the form of a solid timber canopy, erected by ICI to protect the public. Casualties reported so far: Nil.

So famous is the ICI building that, in spite of the American presidential contest and other minor news, Melbourne's morning newspapers both gave large front-page pictures to the building's rather tame strip-tease. Both papers photographed the west wall at a time when, though many others have shattered there was only one pane of glass missing. To the good grey Age *this must have seemed inadequately sensational. The camera, to be sure, cannot lie, but it's wonderful what can be dreamed up in the art department.* Age *readers were shown two missing panes, one a fact and one a re-toucher's figment. As a* Sun *reporter said ruefully afterwards: It was a splendid feat of making two panes of glass go where one blew before.*

All very entertaining. Amusing even. The identity of the 'Spy' was an extremely well-kept secret and remained so. Just as well. Astonishing as it may seem, the 'Spy' and the ICI head of public relations were the same person. This was Peter Ryan unable to resist such a unique, if privileged, opportunity for mischief. Years later some of his mates would chuckle about it when they found out. But the fact remains:

the executive charged with presenting and representing his company's interests had chosen, anonymously, to ridicule and embarrass his employer.

The *Nation* magazine which accommodated the 'Spy' appeared fortnightly as an independent journal of opinion (its own description) between 1958 and 1972. It was founded, edited and owned by Sydney journalist Tom Fitzgerald. And it was said that the magazine offered Australian readers of the time 'fresh and literate perceptions of politics and the economy, manners and morals and the arts'. Fitzgerald was joined by George Munster who wrote for *Nation* under several names (his own included) and contributors such as the art critic Robert Hughes, Clive James, Max Newton and Cyril Pearl. In fact Pearl was the first Melbourne 'Spy' and from the beginning the column had been both provocative and anonymous. When Pearl left Melbourne for Sydney who better to take over from him than his friend Peter Ryan? He would be the Melbourne 'Spy' until the beginning of 1967, stepping aside from time to time for another local insider.

For Ryan the *Nation* commitment marked an early blossoming of sustained freelance writing. Soon he would need his freelance skills and contacts to help pay the family bills. Meantime his portfolio already included a couple of issues of the *Current Affairs Bulletin* for Sydney University, occasional newspaper articles and ABC talks, and some anonymous entries in an encyclopaedia published in Melbourne by the Herald & Weekly Times group. But he was always very proud that Fitzgerald and Munster at *Nation* valued his contribution to the magazine. Nearly 50 years later he admitted to his friend, Max Suich, the Sydney journalist: 'I was never fully comfortable with the "Melbourne Spy". Cyril had long ago introduced the third-person address in which the "Spy" spoke and there was no possibility of breaking it. But it felt affected and twee to me. I've never regarded it a great success. However, a bit of a browse recently leaves me feeling that maybe it wasn't too bad.'

Whatever he was doing (or should not have been doing) Peter Ryan's life would change course while he was at ICIANZ. The trigger was a five-word telegram from Sydney: *Book accepted letter following. Ida.* Angus & Robertson had agreed to publish his wartime memoir *Fear Drive My Feet.* When the book appeared in 1959 the critics thought it was exceptional. The author was recognised as a writer of distinction. E.E. ('Weary') Dunlop, a revered Australian war veteran himself, hailed what he found to be 'a moving account of a young man's lonely heroism in the face of great adversity'.

The title of Ryan's war memoir is from the book of Job, 18.11: *Terrors shall make him afraid on every side, and shall drive him to his feet.*

While Ryan had written his book in 1944–45, it was Ida Leeson (the Ida of the telegram) who finally found a publisher for it. She was a former Mitchell Librarian in

Sydney and had met Ryan during their time at DORCA in Melbourne. Ida Leeson was a house guest of the Ryans when the manuscript surfaced again and its author liked to say Miss Leeson found it while rummaging around the cupboards at 223 Burke Road, Glen Iris. It seems more likely that Davey, who knew where it was, produced it after a dinner table discussion. Ryan himself was quite disheartened about the manuscript's future after knock-backs from three potential publishers. However she got her hands on it, Ida Leeson then did him a great favour. She announced she was taking the manuscript with her back to Sydney and would be showing it to Angus & Robertson. A week or two later—7 August 1957—the good news telegram arrived at the Ryan residence. The book was ready for the Christmas market two years later.

Ryan would later explain: 'I wrote this book at the age of 21, when the travels of 1942 and 1943 were like the day before yesterday. Any small uncertainty—a precise date, the name of a village headman—could be settled from dog-eared notebooks or the tattered sheets of old patrol reports.' The guest of honour at the launch of the book in Melbourne was Sergeant Major Kari of the Royal Papua and New Guinea Constabulary. Kari had appeared often in Ryan's notebooks and patrol reports as the lance-corporal in charge of the native police working with him. Often the young Australian Warrant Officer's safety—even his life—had depended on this brave policeman.

Getting Sergeant Major Kari to Melbourne shortly before Christmas 1959 was no small feat in itself. Yes, he would like to come to Melbourne, but only if someone would collect him in Port Moresby, bring him south and return home with him. Ryan was happy to do that, only to run into a mountain of paperwork from the Port Moresby and Canberra authorities. Paul (later Sir Paul) Hasluck, Australia's Minister for Territories, cleared the way. Ironically Kari had already travelled abroad—to London for the Coronation of Queen Elizabeth in 1953. The man collecting him and escorting him to Melbourne had never been to London and would never go. When he arrived in Port Moresby Ryan told a *South Pacific Post* reporter: 'I've always had a sense of profound gratitude to all my police for their courage and loyalty. I'm glad to be able to take Kari down to Melbourne to share the spotlight as the book is published.' On the flight to Melbourne Ryan and Kari were served a choice of meals with appropriate crockery and cutlery. The last time they had a meal together Ryan recalled, Kari had been drinking tea out of an old bully-beef tin and eating a handful of dried-up rice.

The book was launched at a literary lunch at Melbourne's Hotel Australia where the guests included Ida Leeson, Cyril Pearl and the war correspondent and author Osmar White. Ryan autographed the first copy of *Fear Drive My Feet* for Kari. But the two veterans would have to converse in Pidgin during the week-long visit. Unable to read or write English,

Kari would have to wait until he returned home, where his schoolboy son would read the book to him. Meantime Ryan saw to it that his friend would have a memorable time in Melbourne. Six feet tall and 17 stone (this was 1959, pre-decimal days) the Sergeant Major, in turn, would make quite an impression on Melbourne. He stayed with the Ryans, called on the Lord Mayor and directed traffic in the city while smartly turned out in his navy serge tunic and beret, shorts and sandalled feet. From the observation tower of ICI House, Kari would declare: 'Big fella house too much.'

In the month following the launch *Fear Drive My Feet* was greeted very enthusiastically by reviewers around the country. Douglas Stewart devoted the entire (prestigious) 'Red Page' of the *Bulletin* to it. Ryan's first book, he wrote, had all the clarity of theme and dramatic development that you would hope to find in the best of novels. There were few war books, fact or fiction, in which you would read so tremendous a story. Osmar White, in the Melbourne *Herald*, welcomed 'a great adventure story and, at the same time, a valuable contribution to Australian military history'. White himself had arrived in Port Moresby in 1942 as a war correspondent. His best-known book, *Green Armour*, attracted critical acclaim when it appeared in 1945.

Among the flood of correspondence that arrived at Dalkeith was a generous letter to the author from 'Kem', his one-time boss at the advertising agency. 'I feel ashamed and regretful,' he wrote, 'that you should have worked so closely with me for so long and yet I had not extracted from you more than a fraction of your contribution to your country's service.' A typewritten letter from Miss Anna Bruckner must have surprised and pleased the new author. 'Twenty years ago,' she wrote, 'I was your mother's housekeeper and remember you as a 16- or 17-year-old boy, very friendly and helpful.' Reading *Fear Drive My Feet* had been the highlight of her recent holiday, Miss Bruckner said.

Ryan's book was even mentioned at Question Time in the Senate in Canberra. Had the Minister for Territories seen a copy of *Fear Drive My Feet*, in which allegations were made that certain foreign missionaries in New Guinea assisted the Japanese during the war? The answer to that question was 'No'. But the (unidentified) acting Minister for Territories later confirmed that 39 missionaries of 'enemy alien nationality' from the Territory of New Guinea had been interned in Australia at some stage during the 1939–45 conflict. After the war most of them had returned to the Territory once they received security clearances.

Fear Drive My Feet has rarely been out of print since that time. Editions were subsequently published by Melbourne University Press, Penguin, and Duffy & Snellgrove. Then it appeared again published by Text Classics in Melbourne in 2015. In a powerful introduction, author and academic Peter Pierce described Ryan's by now famous book as 'the finest Australian memoir of war'.

By 1962 the author, 'Spy' and public relations executive

no longer had a day job. Ryan would be unemployed for several months after quitting ICI on a 'point of principle'. It seems an odd thing to do but he quit corporate life over a disagreement about who should work in his department and who should decide that. Odd, too, in that he had no job to go to and a family of four to look after. His saviour (as he called him) was Max Newton, editor of the *Australian Financial Review* at the time. The *AFR* was originally a weekly, then a bi-weekly and from 1963 a daily newspaper. Newton, who would be the founding editor of the *Australian* in 1964, commissioned Ryan to write a series of business and financial articles from Melbourne. This activity and income provided some comfort at a difficult time. As luck would have it (yet again) he would soon have a new job. The best he would ever have, in fact.

Cover picture by Peter Rae, *National Times on Sunday*, 1986.

The Ryan brothers Phillip (left), Peter and Barry.

Above

Teenager at Glen Iris.

Above Right

Ready for work (1940). His first full time job was in the Commonwealth Railways.

M.V. MACDHUI

J. CAMPBELL COMMANDER

MENU

BREAKFAST

Iced Fresh Pineapple in Syrup
Flaked Oats
Granose Biscuits

Corn Flakes
Crispies
Puffed Wheat

San Bran
Vita Brits
Puffed Rice

(With Hot or Cold Milk)

-: FISH :-

Smoked Fillets of Cod, au Beurre

-: ENTREES :-

Saute of Ox Kidney on Toast
Broiled Breakfast Bacon
Cingalese Curry & Rice

-: GRILL :-

Loin Chops & French Fried Potatoes (to order 10 minutes)

Chipped & Mashed Potatoes

TO ORDER (10 minutes)
Eggs Any Style
Omelettes: Plain - Savoury

Cold--Roast Beef

Flannel Cakes with Honey or Golden Syrup
Brown & White Scones

Toast Honey Preserves
Tea Coffee Cocoa

Fruit in Season

6-2-42

ONE COURSE ONLY SERVED ON DECK OR STATE ROOMS

Fine dining on the way to war. (1942)

Left

Lt. Ryan MM. MID. (1945)

Below

Political candidate, Victoria (1947). Despite his enthusiasm he was not successful.

YOUTH SERVED YOU IN WAR . . .
NOW LET IT SERVE YOU IN PEACE.

PETER A. RYAN

- Educated Malvern Grammar School.
- Brilliant Scholastic Career.
- Served in Victorian Crown Law Office.
- Distinguished War Record with A.I.F. — Military Medal and Mentioned in Despatches for Special Intelligence Work.
- Administrative Experience in the Administration of New Guinea.

Vote [1] RYAN FOR TOORAK

THE PROGRESSIVE CANDIDATE

Left

Just married: Davey and Peter. (1947)

Below

Ryan family with house guest Kari from Papua New Guinea and the family Dalmatian, Tally. (1959)

Left

Peter Ryan, PR man. (c 1959)

Below

Old friends atop the ICI building: Sergeant Major Kari and Peter Ryan. (1959)

Melbourne University Press Director. (c 1980)

Country man: Ryan at his property *Rainy Creek* in Victoria's Central Highlands and Goldfields region.

Above

Peter Ryan and Tinker at *Rainy Creek*.

Left

John Spooner caricature of Peter Ryan – *Quadrant* 1993. [From the collection of Sally Guerin]

Above

Peter Ryan at home in North Balwyn. It was a house of books.

Below

The old soldier on ANZAC Day. (2004)

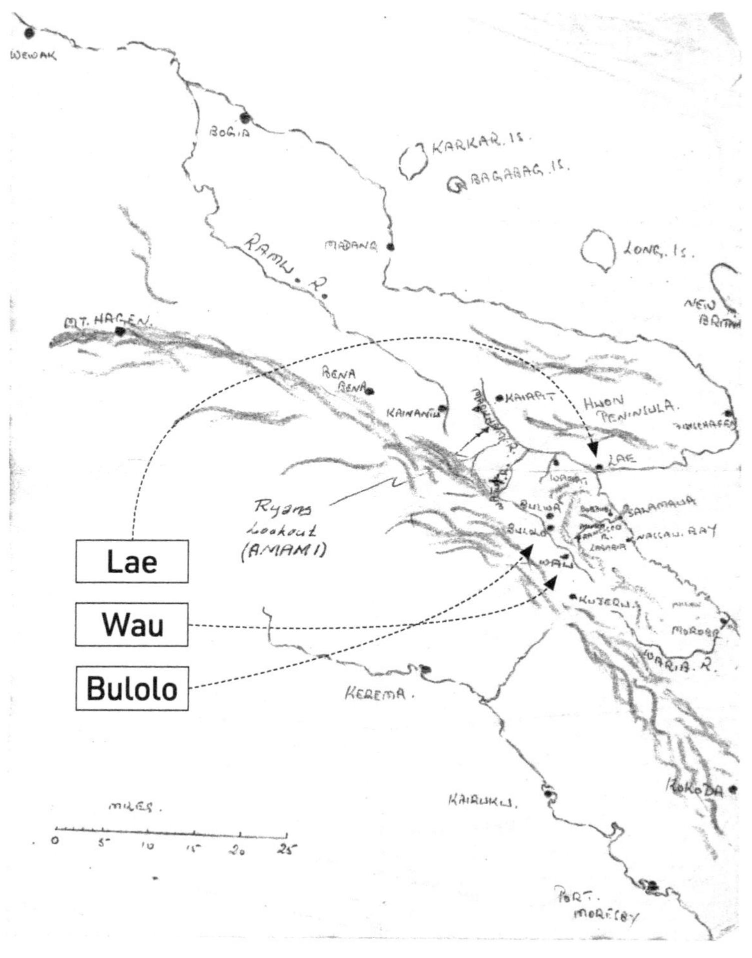

This undated sketch map was drawn by Peter Ryan while on intelligence work in Papua and New Guinea in 1942-1943. It is not to scale. It is likely *Ryan's lookout* (as marked) had a view of the Markham Valley.

4

A REAL BOOKMAN

I would have paid ***them*** *to do the job. There was never a happier employee anywhere.*

Peter Ryan

Nobody ever did Peter Ryan a better turn. He said so himself, long after a suggestion by his friend Creighton Burns led to Ryan's appointment as Director of Melbourne University Press. After months of self-inflicted unemployment he would find himself in a plum job for the next 26 years. A good turn indeed.

In 1961 Burns was a senior lecturer in the political science department at the University of Melbourne where Macmahon Ball was Professor of Political Science. Mac Ball was also chairman of Melbourne University Press, which was looking, without much success, for a new chief executive. The role included a hands-on element as publisher. The job title would be Director. Burns had said, casually, to Mac Ball: 'Ryan could do that job of yours at MUP.' The seed was planted but it would be more than six months before Ryan took up the position.

The appointment required the approval of the University Council and Ryan was first put to work in the office of the Vice Chancellor, Sir George Paton. His assignment, as personal assistant, was to help Sir George produce the University's first triennial submission for funding from the Commonwealth government. It was extremely hard work, he later admitted, 'but in the end no one on that campus had a clearer idea of what was *really* going on—a great asset to the future Director of Melbourne University Press.' Apparently the University of Melbourne was the only one to put in its submission on time. Ryan had passed muster. He already had the confidence of Mac Ball. Now the University Council would approve his appointment.

Melbourne University Press (MUP) had been founded in 1922—a year before Ryan was born—to sell books and stationery to students. In 1923 it published its first book. By the time Ryan arrived, it was the leader in its field.

A study by John Curtain, an academic and a former publisher, found MUP's output from 1961 to 1963 ranked third among Australian book publishers behind Angus & Robertson and F.W. Cheshire and ahead of Rigby Ltd, Jacaranda Press and Lansdowne. The strength of these other presses lay mainly in general and educational publishing. It is clear that under Stanley Addison, its founding manager, and then Frank Wilmot and Gwyn James, MUP had developed as a scholarly press of distinction, and Australia's own. For decades it was the only local university press, before others began to emerge in the 1950s.

Since 1943 MUP had been managed by Gwyn James, an Englishman and academic historian whose talents in every department of book publishing and production were widely admired. Not so his management skills, nor his ability to work effectively with Mac Ball, who would be his last chairman. The net profit of MUP was less than 4,000 pounds and its overdraft had blown out to an alarming 150,000 pounds. Whatever his strengths—he has been described as 'a thinking man's publisher'—James had over-reached, and now effectively demoted, he resigned. Ryan took the new position of Director of the Press (James had been its Manager) on 17 May 1962. He was 38.

What perfect timing. What very good luck. With its international reputation, a respected list and some necessary recent restructuring Melbourne University Press was well positioned for what lay ahead in the 1960s and beyond: continuing post-war prosperity and the great expansion of tertiary education. It would be a golden age for the publishing and newspaper industries. Peter Ryan had the drive, the breadth of interests and the personality that would assure MUP's success, not to mention his own.

The new Director inherited a small empire at MUP—head office, editorial staff, warehouse, printery, bookroom and downtown Melbourne office, distributed over several sites. He was far from impressed with the facilities. Charles Dickens would have been at home in parts of the operation, he said. The printing press was so old-fashioned Caxton could have set up there. Management consultants were called in to advise how such a tenuous, scattered organisation, as he saw it, could be pulled together. Fortunately the new Director also 'inherited' Barbara Ramsden, a University of Melbourne graduate who had worked for the University in different roles since 1928. Later Ryan would say of her: 'Over forty years Miss Ramsden supplied continuity, brains and backbone without which MUP would certainly have sunk.' After assisting the Press for some time, the notoriously formidable, chain-smoking Miss Ramsden joined its staff in 1941. Ryan held her in very high regard. In 1965 she was awarded an MBE for her services. On retirement in 1967 she was honoured by the award of the University Medal. An industry award was named after her.

When Ryan started there the Press's head office was above the National Bank branch on the university campus, behind the Law School. In 1964 it moved to a red brick building in Swanston Street, Carlton, opposite Newman College. Eventually Ryan would get most of the operation—management, editorial, design, sales and production—under one roof in Drummond Street, Carlton. The printery had been closed by then and the bookroom stayed on campus. Early in Ryan's tenure the distinguished

Age writer and author John Hetherington called on him while researching a major series on Australia's publishing houses. He found 'a well set-up man with a plump face, alert blue eyes behind glasses, darkish straight hair and clipped moustache. An entertaining talker with a salty turn of phrase, he has also shown himself to be a good writer in many newspaper and magazine articles; and particularly in a book describing his war experiences, *Fear Drive My Feet*.'

Emboldened by Ryan's new and what he hoped would be secure employment, the family was able to move into a new home that year. After ten years sharing with the aunts this was the first place of their own: a Victorian house at 103 Kooyong Road, Armadale. It needed quite a bit of love and attention which the new owners would provide over the next ten years.

Three 'enduring bequests' from his predecessor greeted the new Director in 1962 and they were still on his mind when he retired 26 years later. One was Manning Clark, whose first book had been printed before Ryan started at MUP and whose sixth and final volume in his *History* series would be published in 1987; another was the MUP bookroom problem of shop-lifting and the third—a happier topic—was the *Australian Dictionary of Biography*.

The Manning Clark 'bequest' was the decision to publish an undetermined number of volumes of Clark's proposed *History of Australia*. Ryan would always claim that Mac Ball had opposed the agreement but was over-ruled. On his arrival at MUP he had found Volume 1 was already printed and an overseas edition pre-sold to Cambridge University Press by his predecessor. Copies (without jackets) were already sitting in the store. A distinctive bright red jacket was designed and produced and would eventually cover all six volumes. It created much interest on bookshop shelves. Ryan would grow increasingly uneasy about the whole project, but from the start it was a significant contributor to the improving financial health of MUP and Ryan would willingly admit that Manning Clark's *History* became and remained an authentic best-seller. It would be another 30 years (when Clark was dead and Ryan had retired from MUP) before Peter Ryan would unleash his forensic and controversial attack on the work and the character of Clark.

The shoplifting 'bequest' remained the most disturbing of the three. Astonishing in fact. Ryan soon discovered that shoplifting was occurring in the bookroom on an alarming scale. In the 1960s Ryan estimated the bookroom, which was the campus bookshop and valuable retail arm of the Press, was losing $250,000 a year to thieves. Most of them were male students and some of them were stealing to order and selling on at a reduced price to other students and commercial customers. After police were called (What! Police on campus!) and some convictions recorded, the University Council ordered MUP to stop the practice of contacting police. In future, miscreants should be reported to university authorities to be disciplined. In an essay on this topic in *Quadrant* Tony

Thomas recalled Ryan's disillusion: 'I feel sad that 26 years' service in the University of Melbourne inspired me with no exalted view of undergraduate idealism or aspiration,' Ryan said. 'This judgement may be unfair, and perhaps unduly influenced by daily exposure to costly and degrading student dishonesty in the bookroom.'

The emergence and great success of the *Australian Dictionary of Biography* had been a welcome 'bequest'. This was the largest long-running project MUP was involved in during the Ryan years. The groundwork at the Melbourne end had been done by Gwyn James and Volume 1 was launched by the Prime Minister, Robert Menzies, in Canberra in 1966. It was a joint venture: the Australian National University chose the entries and prepared the copy for each 'life'; Melbourne University Press handled the design and production of the books and looked after pricing and world-wide sales. The *ADB* was welcomed enthusiastically by scholars and academics, journalists and other reviewers, bookshops and libraries.

As he got to work the first book Ryan published was written by the man who put him up for the MUP job. What was remarkable about *The Tait Case* was that Creighton Burns had been given three weeks to produce a final manuscript. He later described his book as a modest attempt to tell the story of the controversy which followed the Victorian government's decision to hang a man. That man was Robert

Peter Tait, found guilty of the brutal murder of an elderly woman in Melbourne in 1961.

After a great public and legal controversy, the Victorian government commuted the death sentence to one of life imprisonment, never to be released. (Tait died in prison in 1995.) Ryan had approached his old friend with the daunting assignment: the book must be factual, tap into the considerable interest in the case and—one other small thing—had to be completed in three weeks. Burns got the job done on time despite an urgent trip to hospital to remove a kidney stone. There was no truth in the story that he awoke from his operation to find Ryan at his bedside with a pile of proofs to be read. *The Tait Case* attracted good reviews and wide commentary when it appeared simultaneously in hard cover and paperback. Ryan the publisher was on his way.

In those early days the historian Geoffrey Blainey was pleasantly surprised when the new Director (without prompting) raised the royalty from three to ten per cent when his first book was up for a reprint. *The Peaks of Lyell* had been published by Melbourne University Press in 1954 when Blainey was 24 years old. This story of mining in Tasmania remained Ryan's favourite of all the books Blainey would write. He published four more of Blainey's early books, the first of them *The Rush That Never Ended.* Years later Blainey would write of his friend and sometime publisher: 'He did not hesitate to write publicly that he had no time at all for one of my books and little time for this or that chapter in another. You had to respect his even-handed forthrightness.' Ryan more than made up for some of his denunciations with kindness, Blainey added. In a warm tribute after Ryan died, Blainey recalled a man 'fascinated by words and vexed by their misuse'.

In the early 1960s staff recruitment tended to be much less formal than it would later become. Melbourne University Press veteran Sue Hardiman was a case in point. She was 18 at the time and recalled her job interview with the Director: 'At exactly 9.30am Miss Ramsden, the editor, showed me into his office and he introduced himself and his dog [*sic*] and we sat in comfortable chairs. He explained what Melbourne University Press was about and told me what my duties would be. He told me that no job would be too small for me, that you rolled your sleeves up and got on with it. After some little time he offered me the job and asked if I would like to take my coat off and start now.' Not right now was her answer. Hardiman had to give her current employer notice and started at Melbourne University Press a fortnight later. That was November 1964. She stayed until the late 1980s.

Visitors to Ryan's office were often surprised to find a dog dozing by the open fire. The Director enjoyed the company of his dogs in many settings and the one that Miss Hardiman encountered was Dusty, a pure-bred border collie. After Dusty the Director's constant companion was Dr Samuel Johnson (aka Johnson) a border collie kelpie cross. The dogs' master would later wonder: Does there survive in the soul of modern man some faint warm trace of his far ancestor, huddled with his dogs round the comfort of a fire in his cave? Davey Ryan's dog Boswell was a brother of Johnson. The two dogs hated one another.

Of all the people Ryan would hire Michael Cannon was the only one who delivered a manuscript, had his book published and then joined the staff. Cannon's *The Land Boomers* (1966) was an immediate success; indeed a sensation. It documented the greed and corruption that swept gold-rich Victoria during the great land booms of the 19th century. Ryan would later say of it: '*The Land Boomers* in full and dreadful detail dared to tell a story which our professional historians had preferred not to notice.' Cannon worked closely with Ryan for a time as Assistant Director, trouble-shooting in the printing, bookroom and trade departments.

In 1966 MUP also produced a small publication entitled *The Preparation of Manuscripts.* It was written by the Director in his most helpful and professional frame of mind and ranged over topics from headings and footnotes to copyright and consistency. The relationship between an author and publisher *ought* to be one of the most agreeable and rewarding associations known to mankind, he wrote. Nothing helped to establish such a friendship more than an accurate and thoughtfully prepared manuscript. Not long afterwards Oxford University Press published a monograph by Ryan that he had been thinking about for years. It reviewed the life of Sir Redmond Barry, founder and first chancellor of the University of Melbourne, a founder of the Victorian State Library and the judge in the trial of Ned Kelly.

No other city in Australia has had a benefactor to compare with Sir Redmond, Ryan wrote. A revised edition appeared later (in 1980) under the imprint of Melbourne University Press. One reviewer noted the author's 'trademark economy of language'. Another thought this short study of Barry was a wholesome corrective 'for the Kelly devotees among your friends'.

A benefactor whose vision and generosity directly benifited Melbourne University Press was Sir Wilfred Russell Grimwade. Sir Russell was a chemist, botanist, businessman, philanthropist and collector of books and art. 'Miegunyah' was the name of the Grimwade family mansion in Orrong Road, Toorak, and Miegunyah Press is today a special imprint of Melbourne University Press that publishes prestigious books and is funded by the Grimwade bequest. The imprint was established and secured on Ryan's watch at MUP when Miegunyah Press No. 1 appeared with great fanfare in 1967. This was a scholarly biography of Sir Russell by Professor John Poynter. The author is a distinguished historian and was a long-time chairman of the MUP board and later a deputy vice chancellor of the University.

Sir Russell had died 12 years earlier. This first publication was paid for by the Press and was launched at Miegunyah; Sir Robert Menzies, no longer Prime Minister of Australia and now Chancellor of the University, did the honours. The long invitation list included academics and historians, politicians, journalists and friends of the Grimwade family. The beautifully designed and produced book attracted much interest and as the function went on Ryan took his young and rather nervous secretary, Sue Hardiman, aside. She was told to 'walk around' the throng and make discreet suggestions about return of, or payment for, copies that were being examined. It was a useful lesson for the future: always ensure that books are autographed *after* they have been paid for.

There were no further Miegunyah Press releases until after Peter Ryan retired in 1988. Ryan had done everything he could to ensure that the Press would benefit in full from the Miegunyah bequest, but there were long delays in finalising details of this gift and eventually, as Ryan had feared, the Press did not fare quite as well as it had expected.

By now it had long dawned on son and daughter Andrew and Sally Ryan that their home life was rather different from that enjoyed by many of their friends. Andrew recalled 'no sport, no religion and an absent father most week-nights'. But weekends were for family and from the time Andrew could walk, father and son would go horse riding at least one day of the weekend. After Sally arrived she would join her father and brother riding in the bush, where the billy was boiled and Davey followed in the family station wagon, with some exotic luncheon dish or other. While out there the children learned how to tie knots, light fires safely, read a map and other practical bush skills. On the home front, however, Sally said that Davey had done all the heavy lifting with schooling, friends and other activities—'a marvellous job on a shoestring budget'.

Despite Ryan's absences during the week he would regularly take the family to dinner. 'I didn't know any other kids who went to Florentino, the Latin, Society and other places with such regularity,' Andrew said. 'I think the first time I visited Florentino I was in my pyjamas and dressing gown.' The children also met a constant stream of visitors and fellow diners who fascinated them: people like Mac Ball, Creighton Burns, Geoffrey and Ann Blainey, Michael Cannon and B.A. Santamaria.

When Andrew left school his father gave him $200 and a return air ticket to Papua New Guinea where he spent most of 1970. Father and son were reunited at one point and together visited Wau, Bulolo and the Markham area where Warrant Officer Ryan had served in World War Two. They celebrated their 19th birthdays up there, in starkly different circumstances: one in 1970, the other in 1942.

For the rest of his long life Peter Ryan maintained a close interest in the development of Papua New Guinea and a warm regard for its people. Time and time again in a wide range of venues and publications he would stress Australia's great debt to them. After the war he made at least 29 visits to Port Moresby and beyond, funding a school, visiting and helping old friends, and researching scores of articles on the country's problems and progress. His greatest gift to them would be the *Encyclopaedia of Papua and New Guinea.*

This very large and remarkable publication took MUP five years to plan and compile. Ryan had the idea under the shower one morning and the editorial board that was assembled was chaired by the Nobel Prize winning scientist Sir Frank Macfarlane 'Mac' Burnet. Ryan volunteered to be General Editor and in the end there were contributions by more than 200 experts from around the world. But in those pre-computer days there was a last-minute hitch: The index for this three-volume work was complex and critical and its creator fell ill. Sally Ryan was drafted in to get the job done, with expert advice from Miss Ramsden and others at MUP. It took four weeks during which time many hundreds of index cards were carefully laid out around the Ryan household. Much of the third volume comprised that index, 83 pages of it. The *Encyclopaedia of Papua and New Guinea* was published by Melbourne University Press in association with the new University of Papua and New Guinea. It was launched in Port Moresby in March 1972 but Ryan was not present. He was in hospital in Melbourne after some emergency surgery.

In one sense the encyclopaedia that he had imagined was a sort of Domesday Book for the people of Papua New

Guinea on the eve of their Independence (which came in 1975). Certainly it captured this rugged and fascinating country at one historic point in time: its past and its physical, social and economic characteristics. The encyclopaedia was very well received, locally and internationally, by reviewers and university libraries. Andrew Peacock, Australia's Minister for External Territories at the time, wrote to Peter Ryan: 'The breadth and scholarship of this work are of the highest quality.'

From the mid-1970s Ryan inhabited two worlds each week: one in town, Monday to Friday, working at MUP, dining and socialising; the other in the country at the weekend which was a time for family, for riding, for building a house. It was a routine shared fully with only one other party—his dog. In the mid-1960s the Ryans had bought a small property with a rundown farmhouse on the edge of the town of Romsey, about 60 kilometres north of Melbourne. They kept horses there and Ryan maintained an impressive vegetable garden.

Then in 1974 Peter and Davey bought Rainy Creek, a property at Tooborac in central Victoria about 90 kilometres north of Melbourne. It would be their retreat of choice for nearly 30 years. Rainy Creek was a 20-acre block (8 hectares) and Ryan ran some pampered livestock and three indulged horses, one of them quite ancient. Building a new house there was a family venture; a local builder put down the basic structure and Peter (a good bush carpenter) and the other three worked long and hard at the rest. While this was going on they all lived in a small pre-fabricated shed on the property, sleeping bags lined up in a row, dog and cat at their feet. A close family, you could say. Once the house itself could be lived in Ryan refused to have a telephone there and when he finally relented one was installed in the shed. It was kept in an old biscuit tin so anyone around the place could hear it ring. Distinctively.

The Ryan city residence by this time was in North Carlton. But when Andrew and Sally moved out Peter and Davey bought a small cottage in Flemington, near the freeway end of the drive from Rainy Creek.

Davey lived at the farm, usually travelling to the city mid-week for dinner with Peter and often the children. Peter spent the working week in the city and joined her in the country at weekends. It was an arrangement that suited them both. Particularly him.

In 1978 Wendy Sutherland joined Melbourne University Press as managing editor. She had come from Oxford University Press, 'swapping an O for an M', she would say. Sutherland described her new boss as 'a real bookman', and found him invariably good humoured *except* when jobs ran late or he encountered incompetence. She particularly admired the literary interests and background that he brought to his role. Sutherland attended weekly Press meetings with production and finance managers and chaired by the Director. These were carefully focused, well run and rarely took more than 20 minutes.

Nick Walker, who in the 1980s was the Assistant Director: Publishing at the Press, has a clear-eyed view of his former colleague's management style. 'It was of its era,' he recalled. 'He was the Director and as such he delegated and judged. Those who did their job well were approved of and secure. Those who didn't, or who challenged Peter's authority, were to be dealt with—and one knew it.'

Max Suich—ultimately editor in chief of the Sydney newspapers and magazines of the Fairfax group—was often in Melbourne on business. MUP, he recalled as a great place to drop in for a yarn and invariably a warm welcome from Ryan, his secretary and his dog. Often he and Ryan would make a tour of inspection where Suich would see new and handsome volumes about to go out and they would discuss upcoming books. 'Peter was a true publisher in the sense that the edited manuscript wasn't the end of the business but the start … the type, the printer, the printery, the margins, the binding and the illustrations were all fully and neatly considered. His stories of his authors were always entertaining, often ribald, sometimes side-splitting.' When the two of them went out to dinner—perhaps Florentino, maybe the Latin—Ryan's dog went in the back of the ute and waited for the diners without complaint. The warm friendship between the two men continued until Ryan's death in 2015. A few years later Suich explained: 'His gift to me was a front row seat at one of the roles he played in life

... arch raconteur of the city of Melbourne and its denizens of all types, astringent critic, mischievous prankster, master storyteller of the well-crafted anecdote of the academic and legal worlds.'

It had been Suich who sent the then unpublished writer Blanche d'Alpuget to see Ryan with what would be her first book. This was a biography of Sir Richard Kirby, a long-term President of the Australian Commonwealth Conciliation and Arbitration Commission. Ryan accepted it straight away on the strength of a couple of chapters and an outline. Then, said d'Alpuget, the Director proved to be a magnificent mentor. He gave her the Press's style manual and wrote weekly letters of encouragement. 'On one occasion he drew a picture of me being guillotined for some misdemeanour with style,' she recalled. After writing *Mediator: A Biography of Sir Richard Kirby*, d'Alpuget went on to become an acclaimed novelist, biographer (famously of Bob Hawke) and essayist. She has never forgotten the help Peter Ryan gave her. 'Whenever his name has come up—at literary festivals for example—I have always acknowledged the great gift he bestowed on me,' she said. 'He was a dream publisher for a young author.'

Surviving copies of memos from the Ryan years at MUP show he took the business of publishing, and of being a professional publisher, *very* seriously. His own interests in biography, history and literature, in particular, fitted neatly and happily with the natural strengths of the Press in these areas. Importantly, these memos also show that Ryan was a canny manager of his board, an essential ingredient in the advancement, even survival, of an institutionally owned enterprise. He understood the need for MUP to be kept free of influences—bureaucratic, personal and political—prevalent in his own and at other universities. Ryan knew that freedom for the professional publisher had to be fought for and won. As one close observer of those days put it: 'Ryan's quarter century at the helm of the press is littered with evidence of skirmishes and artful manoeuvres, most of which were probably necessary.' The new Director had managed to 'unhook' MUP operations like hiring and firing and administration from the University; in short the day-to-day running of the business, but the University retained ultimate control as it appointed the Melbourne University Press board. Professor John Poynter was chairman of that board for eleven years of Ryan's management. Later on Poynter would say: 'I learned how economically the Director and a handful of trusted colleagues managed the organisation, how meticulously he briefed the board and its various committees and how shrewdly he negotiated legal agreements.'

The relative independence that Ryan managed to secure for Melbourne University Press delivered valuable benefits for the Director personally: the freedom for him to do a great deal of private writing; and the opportunity to conduct a writing and ideas salon in the city's best restaurants.

However, the interests of MUP came first.

It is not usual now, nor was it then, for a busy publisher to be an active freelance writer at the same time. Ryan managed both. In fact he liked to think of himself as a writer, first of all. The delayed success of *Fear Drive My Feet* had been a great confidence booster as had the interest sparked by his mysterious 'Melbourne Spy' column in *Nation* magazine. Ryan was subsequently, and anonymously, the 'Melbourne Oyster' in the *Australian Financial Review*. This was a restaurant column and hence a subject to which he could bring considerable authority and a great deal of practical experience. There was also a column—this one under his own name—in the *Australian*, though he was fired, on the instructions, he claimed, of the newspaper's proprietor, Rupert Murdoch. It was an item about the stockbroker and businessman Sir Cecil Looker that caused his downfall. The editor who gave him his marching orders was the widely respected Adrian Deamer, who was dismissed himself a few hours later. Ryan felt a perverse pleasure in being first out the door that day.

Throughout his MUP years and later the Director was also a prolific book reviewer, appearing in the *Age*, the *Sydney Morning Herald* and the *Weekend Australian*. Other outlets included smaller publications like *News Weekly*, *Nation*, *Australian Book Review* and *Quadrant*. Ryan once told an interviewer, 'I do book reviews when anybody is kind enough to send me a book.' Then he added: 'I'll go further than that. I'm abject enough to importune literary editors for books to review.' No subject seemed to be off limits but his output included reviews of a wide range of biographies—Winston Churchill, Boswell, Thomas More, Bertrand Russell and Sir Francis Drake among them. There was only one thing he asked of any publication he was writing for: spike it (don't publish it) by all means, but don't alter it.

By the 1970s, Ryan had become increasingly conservative in his political views but he voted for the first Whitlam Labor government and readily admitted so. Its actions in Papua New Guinea proved to be a particular disappointment to him: self-government in 1973 and independence in 1975. He was in no doubt that what he termed the 'premature ditching of its responsibilities' would prove to be one of the costliest policy blunders Australia ever made. Ryan believed Papua New Guinea was pushed into independence about 10 years too early and before the public service had a chance to properly develop; and hence the country's continuing problems with corruption and crooked politicians.

After a long spell as Washington correspondent for the *Age*, Ryan's friend Creighton Burns returned home and was appointed editor of the newspaper in 1981. The pair would spend a lot of time together, particularly at the Melbourne Savage Club. Ryan would soon have a new and regular vehicle for his views on subjects ranging from Papua New Guinea to rural life in country Victoria. He called his column, with a nod to George Orwell, 'As I Please.' A couple of editors later and after a run of seven years this association (like his earlier one at the *Australian*) would end abruptly. By then the writer would have retired from Melbourne University Press.

In 1983 the *Age* published 'Ryan's Niugini', a four-part series assessing the post-independence situation in PNG. The main purpose of his trip, with Davey, had been to see old wartime friends. That part was a great pleasure. He also found much that disturbed him, particularly political corruption and a justice system in serious trouble. There was a dramatic opportunity for an eye-witness report, subsequently published in the *Age*: 'My wife and I made early acquaintance with both crime and the police. Within 24 hours of reaching Port Moresby we were held up at pistol point, knocked down and robbed.'

None of this would shake Ryan's commitment to the country and its people. His view remained that the terrible burdens Australia had placed on the indigenous people during World War Two left us with a great debt of honour that must be paid—no matter what. In the *Age* he pointed out: 'Our victories were won and Australia saved by the astounding help and sacrifice of the Papuans and New Guineans.' They were not yet one people.

Throughout the Ryan years at MUP his lunching habits were truly legendary. In fact they had been since he left university—places like the Old White Hart Hotel, opposite Parliament House and now long gone, and the Society restaurant with companions like Cyril Pearl, Robin Boyd and Michael Cannon. Ryan got to know Bill Ingram, the doorman at Melbourne's Florentino, so well that he devoted an entire essay to him in his book *Brief Lives.* Ingram held the job (*performed* might be more accurate) for 20 years and was 'one of the most perfect gentlemen I ever knew'. The Ingram that Ryan admired was quietly spoken, discreet and polite with no trace of servility. After one lunch Ryan's guest, a very senior police officer, tried a little joke as the pair left the restaurant. On being handed his hat he told Ingram: 'That's not mine.' Ryan, much amused, heard the doorman reply: 'I'm sorry to hear that Sir because it's the one you came in with.'

It was at the Latin restaurant in Lonsdale Street where the most enthusiastic lunching was done—serious eating, drinking and animated conversation from which ideas for books sometimes emerged. The Director's table for two in the corner for 12.30pm was a regular Friday booking. By 1.30pm the table for two was often a table for six, eight or more. Mac Ball might be there, or Creighton Burns who had slipped away from his duties at the *Age.* If Mac Ball was there, former students of his might join the table; politicians like Andrew Peacock and Tony Staley and the writer and political activist B.A. Santamaria. Asked once who he would select as a sole companion on a desert island, Ryan reckoned it would be Santamaria, 'for his mind'. On Friday nights, after a long lunch, Ryan would appear at the Celtic

Club (since closed).

As it still does, Melbourne had four well-established Gentlemen's Clubs in those days: the Melbourne Club, the Athenaeum, the Australian Club and the Melbourne Savage Club. Curiously, Ryan was not a member of any of them. He would have made an ideal 'Savage' given that club's bohemian origins and he often lunched as the guest of Creighton Burns at its elegant premises in Bank Place.

McCoppins Wine Bar in Fitzroy was another Ryan favourite. Mark Sheehan, who worked there when he was a university student, remembers Ryan clearly because of his striking attire: 'what I now know to be a neckerchief, red and white or blue and white in a distinctive pattern'. It was always a good way of getting the bar staff's attention, Sheehan said.

The journalist Rowan Callick once wrote of Ryan's eyes being 'bright with mischief'. They certainly were. This was a man with a quirky sense of humour, a quick and often biting wit. A man who seemed to be naturally mischievous. Quite often his mischief making was in a restaurant setting, a stunt in New Guinea among the most notable. Peter and Andrew Ryan had turned up for dinner at the Bulolo Hotel clad in clean shirts, shorts, long socks and shoes; normal dress, except on Saturday night when long trousers were required. They were turned away. Father and son had only one pair of long trousers between them so Peter put them on, checked in to the dining room and took a table near a window. Then he removed the trousers, passed them out the window to his son who put them on, walked inside and took his place at the table. After that it was simply a matter of removing them (Andrew wore shorts underneath) and passing them, under the table, to his father who put them back on. A convivial dinner followed. Nobody mentioned (maybe even noticed) that Andrew was wearing shorts as the pair left the dining room that night.

Mischief on an even greater scale played out at a North Melbourne restaurant on April Fools' Day, 1981. No fewer than seven women, most of them unknown to one another, were invited to dinner by Ryan at one of his favourite haunts, The Great Australian Bite. Each thought it was dinner for two. All were surprised to find a table set for ten. Then their host arrived with an eighth guest, Professor John Poynter, Chairman of the MUP board. He, too, was surprised to find he was sharing the occasion with others. One or two who attended later recalled that an agreeable evening was had by all. The tenth place at the table remained empty. Perhaps it was never allocated. Maybe the guest failed to turn up. If it was part of Ryan's elaborate joke he never let on who (if anyone) was supposed to fill that empty seat. This was a man who sought out and enjoyed the company of women; and plenty of women, in turn, found his company and attention entertaining or flattering. Sometimes both. Asked at the Savage Club one day how his social life was going he joked: 'I'm so busy I've been thinking of putting a boy on.'

By the 1980s Melbourne University Press had achieved, in the Director's words, comparative stability and security. While there was no rolling five-year plan, or similar, Ryan and his board were publishing between 30 and 40 titles a year. That list was heavily populated by history, biography and military books, the last being largely biography. Gordon 'Cactus' Connell was represented. Forty years after he taught Ryan the schoolboy at Malvern Grammar School, Ryan the MUP Director published *The Mystery of Ludwig Leichhardt*. When Ryan wrote to Connell to confirm his 'bijou mystery' would be published he told him the MUP board had deducted half a mark for lack of neatness. That was in 1980. As things turned out it would be quite a big year for Leichhardt studies at Melbourne University Press.

It was widely recognised that Manning Clark's *History of Australia*, six volumes in the end, and the *Australian Dictionary of Biography* were two very profitable titles. Among others were Geoffrey Serle's *Monash* and a matriculation-level Chemistry textbook which for a time had that market largely to itself. Ryan would say, with some exaggeration, that his list showed a reasonable spread over all branches of knowledge where manuscripts were available.

When, from time to time, a promising scientific idea was put forward he was keen to do something with it. He was immensely proud of *The Insects of Australia*, a joint undertaking with the CSIRO. It took five years to complete with its 3,000 illustrations and more than 1,000 pages of text and artwork. But science publishing was not front of mind at Ryan's MUP. Nor did he develop an Education division, as some other scholarly publishers were doing, to exploit the booming textbook market.

Near the end of his life, in his publishing memoir *Final Proof* (2010), Ryan explained the progress (or otherwise) of manuscripts at MUP. It was the MUP board which made the basic decision whether a newly offered manuscript was 'in' or 'out'. To do this it could draw on a wide range of specialists around the University and elsewhere for advice. 'In my whole service,' Ryan wrote, 'I never saw a submission accepted because of outside influence or pressure; nor a sound piece of work rejected merely because it might offend somebody important.' No doubt this was true, and he was, of course, vetting the submissions that went to his board.

There was no system and no pattern in the manner that manuscripts came to MUP for consideration. Sometimes they had been nurtured by the Director, as had happened with Geoffrey Serle's acclaimed biography of Sir John Monash. But usually, Ryan said, they just seemed to drop from heaven. As they well might, given the position and reputation of Melbourne University Press at that time. Take, for example, the case of Elsie Webster and her remarkable manuscript that had arrived at MUP one day 'out of the silence'. Ryan devoted an entire chapter of *Final Proof* to what would prove to be something of a publishing event. Miss Webster was a private scholar, indeed a very private person, a scholar of genius, Ryan believed. She had not been to university. What she had produced was a 275,000-word manuscript (she typed it herself) on Ludwig Leichhardt. It had taken her 15 years to complete. But it was not a conventional biography. Ryan, who thought it was a masterpiece, said it described the fate of the great adventurer in the 100 years or so since he disappeared into the interior of Australia. Miss Webster's book *Whirlwinds in the Plain: Ludwig Leichhardt—Friends, Foes and History*, created a minor sensation when it appeared in 1980. To its publisher's great pleasure, he said, *Whirlwinds* was glowingly reviewed by scholars worldwide; success with the reading public was attested by solid sales in the bookshops and by numerous literary awards.

While Melbourne University Press was a valued member of the Melbourne University family its Director was very proud of the authors he brought in (or who walked in) from outside. Ryan's board chairman for eleven years, Professor John Poynter, noted: 'Towards Melbourne University itself and to the academic world of the day generally, he was always ambivalent.' Ambivalent may have been putting it generously. Ryan could be hostile as demonstrated in a letter he wrote to the *Age* of 22 May 1984.

On that occasion he unleashed a withering attack on 23 members of his own university's history department. This large group had written to the *Age* a few days earlier dissociating themselves from recent comments on Asian immigration by Professor Geoffrey Blainey, a colleague. Blainey had 'accidentally' (as the *Australian Financial Review* put it) initiated a debate on Asian immigration. The story broke after a low-key address to a Rotary Club convention in the provincial city of Warrnambool. Blainey had criticised the Hawke government over the pace of immigration at the time and said the influx of Asian migrants was perceived as too large for public opinion to handle. His remarks were first reported in Warrnambool's daily newspaper, the *Standard.*

In their letter to the *Age* Blainey's colleagues said his raising of the immigration issue, 'however much it is couched in the language of reason, becomes an invitation to less responsible groups to incite feelings of racial hatred'. Their letter added that Professor Blainey had been speaking and writing on this issue as an individual and not as a representative of historians at the University of Melbourne.

Conceding that Blainey needed no help in a scrap. Ryan waded in anyway in support of a man he liked and whose work he admired. Cut back to its bare bones, he wrote, the academics' letter had made three points:

> Some subjects are too dangerous for a democracy to discuss freely.
>
> Even discussion in reasonable language might be too heady for ordinary taxpayers.
>
> The deep wisdom of academic persons allows them to pronounce for all of us.

Ryan summed up his disgust: 'In short, these immensely knowledgeable nannies will take us all kindly by the hand and shepherd us around the nasty things which the rest of us are too immature to see.' Nobody would ever accuse Peter Ryan of mincing his words. His letter appeared in the *Age* under the heading: WISE NANNIES.

Ryan suffered a personal setback himself the following year. The Ryan cottage in Flemington was burgled but the only items of value taken were his treasured war medals. They were replaced by authorities in Australia and the UK after much correspondence and a Statutory Declaration by their owner. In 1986 the stolen medals turned up, without explanation, in Ryan's letterbox. They were wrapped in newspaper and arrived just before Anzac Day. Was a guilty conscience at work? Whatever the explanation the old soldier was very pleased to have his medals back.

As his long tenure at MUP was drawing to a close Ryan had another revealing spat with the academy—this time the Australian National University in Canberra. He was asked to contribute to the final volume of a bicentennial history of Australia that the ANU was producing and he did so. In fact he thought it might have been the best piece of writing he had ever produced. His essay was not published. So he sent it to Robert Haupt, editor of the *National Times on Sunday*, who confirmed Ryan's view when he responded: 'I think this is the best thing you have ever written.' Haupt published it soon after as a major exclusive, 'The End of the Dreamtime'. Several other papers and journals picked it up and Ryan shared the George Watson Essay Prize for work undertaken in 1986. The author was never given an explanation for the original rejection; finally a phone call he made had established that the piece would not be used. Clearly the Ryan essay had not been what the editors had in mind. Looking back over his life (he was in his sixties by now) the author had found much to celebrate and a great deal that concerned him: 'What I can make out fills me with unease—even grief,' he wrote. 'It hints that my country has run out of luck; that it lacks the nerve and purpose for the huge exertions which alone might save Australia from being thrown, a discarded disappointment, into the dustbin of early 21st century history.'

According to Ryan, between the 1920s and the 1980s a great change of character had occurred in ordinary Australians: They had become, as individuals, less able to help either themselves or others. Turning to the education system, he hoped for one that produced 'useful, rounded, modern minds, instead of one creating resentful illiterates'. As for himself: it was comforting, he said, that by the year 2000 he would probably be dead. He got that bit wrong.

Before he retired from MUP Ryan received some encouraging advice from Warren Perry, a fellow historian, former soldier and writer. Perry had written to him after reading a 'brilliant piece of political analysis' Ryan had produced on the Whitlam government: 'When you retire you must take with you a large bottle of ink and a good pen and not allow yourself to rust away in inactivity. You are the William Hazlitt of today.'

Of course Ryan had no plans to 'rust away'. But he did slip away quietly, if reluctantly, from MUP when his compulsory retirement date came round at the end of 1988. The Director's departure was marked by one small, indeed puzzling, hiccup of his own making. Vintage Ryan behaviour you might say. At his final board meeting he had been presented with an illuminated address signed by those present; and a rare—and surely much appreciated—copy of Samuel Johnson's *Journey to the Hebrides.* Some time later Ryan parcelled up these gifts and returned them to the University. We will never know what had *really* upset him. In *Final Proof* he said they were returned when he learned that his friend Michael Cannon had not been appointed to replace him. He even used the term 'betrayal'.

There must have been more to it than that. Given that Michael Cannon was 59 years old when Ryan retired it was never likely he would have been appointed by a board intent on change; one planning to review MUP's financial and managerial relationship with the University and hence the relative independence it had enjoyed under Ryan. Cannon was not one of those interviewed for the job at the beginning and as the process dragged on it might have been Ryan who proposed him. It probably was. But Peter Ryan had held that job for 26 years so of course the board would be looking far and wide for the right person to take MUP into a different future. Ryan must have understood that. Much as he loved that place (and he really did) the decision on his replacement was actually none of his business. Nor should it have been. (In the next 26 years Melbourne University Press would have no fewer than six Directors—only one of them was a woman, and one filled the position on two separate occasions.)

Enormous change—not least technological—lay ahead for the Australian publishing industry. Peter Ryan had made his own considerable contribution and was now moving on. While Melburne University Press was in his care he had extended its reach and further enhanced its reputation. Ryan's MUP was a model university press of its day.

5

MUCH MORE TO DO

There are few sweeter writers in this country. His political pieces have the clarity and toughness of Orwell; his musings on bush life have a perfection of form reminiscent of E.B. White.

Les Carlyon

It is not easy to begin a new career at 65, particularly when you lack the professional qualifications expected for the job. Peter Ryan did. Almost 50 years after his hopes of becoming a solicitor had been dashed the veteran publisher was appointed an officer of the Supreme Court of Victoria. His new job: Secretary to the Board of Examiners for Legal Practitioners.

Ryan started in his new position in October 1988 shortly after retiring from Melbourne University Press. But for the previous five years he had been a part-time member of the Victorian Solicitors' Disciplinary Tribunal and the experience had stirred his interest in administration of the law and legal ethics. As retirement approached Ryan sought the advice of Supreme Court Judge Bernard Teague. Did he know of any positions around the court or legal profession for someone with no legal background or qualifications? The Judge had replied: 'Are you serious? They are desperately trying to get a Secretary for the Board of Examiners for Legal Practitioners.' (In 1987 Mr Justice Teague had been the first solicitor appointed to the Supreme Court of Victoria. He had served on the Board of Examiners himself from 1974 to 1987.)

It was most unusual for a non-lawyer to be appointed Secretary of the Board of Examiners and Ryan was probably the first. He had studied law for one year only at the University of Melbourne before specialising in history. Among the previous incumbents was Sir George Paton, former Dean of the Law School and later Vice Chancellor of the University. This was the Sir George Paton whom Ryan had worked with closely before being confirmed as Director of Melbourne University Press in 1962. Ryan's irregular background proved no obstacle in the end. The Chief Justice, Sir John Young, was consulted and the new Secretary was appointed on a six-month trial. He stayed for 15 years.

The board Ryan served comprised barristers and solicitors and usually Victoria's Attorney-General and Solicitor-General. The Secretary's office had a 'watch-dog' function but its chief purpose was to help all properly qualified candidates through the admission process. It was the board that approved an applicant's Articles, provided they were in order. A year later, when it was time for admission to the profession, it would sign a Board Certificate if it was satisfied the candidate was 'in all respects qualified'. Writing in the *Law Institute Journal* Ryan explained to students: 'Entering into articles of clerkship can be compared to entering the straight in a race: the winning post is in sight, but there is still the chance of tripping; the last stretch still demands your full concentration and effort.' Ryan found the work very busy at times, stimulating and pleasant. He enjoyed mixing with the students, with lawyers and judges. 'I like the job,' he told one interviewer. 'It keeps me mentally on my toes all the time.'

One of the few items that moved from MUP in Carlton to the Board of Examiners' chambers at the Supreme Court was Clifton Pugh's portrait of Sir John Kerr. It was the second time Ryan had offered it a safe haven. The portrait was being painted by Pugh on 11 November 1975, the day Sir John dismissed the Whitlam Government. Ryan's old army colleague, now Governor-General of Australia, had interrupted a sitting with Pugh at Government House in Canberra to sign the warrant dismissing the government. When Pugh heard the news he packed up his paints and hardboard and left, reportedly in a rage.

Ryan thought Pugh's near life-size portrait of Sir John was 'stupendous'. It was sold privately to two business partners and began its public life at Melbourne's Café Latin. So it was,

Ryan wrote, 'that Sir John took a place of temporary honour at the Latin, gravely supervising the service of spaghetti and scaloppine at lunch time and at dinner'. New owners at the restaurant decided it must go and at short notice Ryan offered what he called 'emergency hospitality' in the foyer of his office at MUP. The portrait attracted a great deal of interest and comment (as Ryan would have intended) and it was said that every year on 10 November he would turn Sir John to the wall in case someone attempted to do him a mischief the following day. By then the dismissal was ten years ago but the portrait's guardian 'marvelled at the heat and horror it could still arouse'. With the agreement of its owners Ryan removed the portrait from MUP to the court. It amused him that Sir John looked down on applicants to practise law in Victoria. The experience would do them no harm, he thought, particularly those who might pursue a career in constitutional law.

As he settled into his new 'day job' Ryan was also entering an extremely productive period as a writer. Over the next 25 years there would be six more books, newspaper columns, articles and reviews, papers at conferences and a remarkable body of work for *Quadrant*.

The first of the books followed two brief research visits in 1989 to the remote Mount Kare goldmine in Papua New Guinea. *Black Bonanza: A landslide of gold* was published in 1991. Ryan told the tumultuous story of the first gold rush in the history of Papua New Guinea; one that was almost exclusively 'an affair of the indigenous people'. It is a tale of the extraordinary riches that followed the opening of the mine; and the violence, drunkenness, disease, theft and corruption which marked everyday life there. Ryan reckoned it was a 'hair-raisingly good yarn about human beings and what they will do when they get the scent of gold in their nostrils'. The mine was in wild mountainous country about 600 kilometres north of Port Moresby and was probably the site of the world's first helicopter-serviced gold rush. Mining specialists and visitors like Ryan flew in; the locals—and many from afar—walked in. The fact that the author was still fluent in Pidgin helped him enormously as he went about his research. Peter Ryan dedicated the book:

> *To my valued friend Sergeant Major Kari, LSM, of the old Royal Papua and New Guinea Constabulary; and to his people—'ol man-meri-pikinini'—the ordinary men, women and children of Papua New Guinea among whom and through whose help I grew to be a man.*

When the author returned to Mount Kare at the end of 1990 a conventional mining camp was springing up. How different it all was. Gone was 'the seething colour, the pulsating life of thousands of miners and their families gouging uncertain livings from the mud'. The transformation to mechanical mining was well underway.

Rowan Callick was also familiar with the story. As he explained in the *Australian Financial Review*: 'There is no question about the most extraordinary story I have covered as a journalist: the 1988–90 gold rush in which 10,000 Papua New Guinea Highlanders clawed $400 million of nuggets from the muddy slopes of Mount Kare.' Ryan's book was a splendidly thorough account of that rush, he said. Callick and Ryan first met in Papua New Guinea where Callick worked from 1976 to 1986 as a freelance journalist and as manager of a locally owned newspaper, magazine and printing company. As Callick recalled: 'I had met Peter several times on his visits to Moresby where he had sought me out, and we had got on pretty well. He was fascinated that one of our core papers was *Wantok*, a weekly newspaper published in *Tok Pisin* (Pidgin).'

When Callick settled in Australia, he said Ryan 'took him on as a project', helping him to settle in, introducing him to interesting and useful people. Part of that long induction were regular lunches at the Latin and Society restaurants. Callick understood his friend's immense and continuing loyalty to the people of Papua New Guinea and appreciated his wide range and depth of interests. The Peter Ryan he got to know was 'a dapper figure yet there was something raffish about him. And he was very much his own man: anyone who thinks he was part of some elite would be mistaken.'

Ryan's newspaper column *As I Please* survived a change of editor at the *Age* in 1989. His friend for more than 40 years, Creighton Burns, had resigned for family reasons after eight years in the job and was replaced by Mike Smith. The new editor liked Ryan's material and made one major change: the column that had appeared fortnightly since 1986 would henceforth be published weekly. While the *Age* columnist was fully employed by day at the Board of Examiners, a letter he wrote (in 1993) outlines his *modus operandi* as a freelance writer as well: 'Can I point out that *As I Please* began exactly seven years ago; that it always had top priority in my commitments; that the writing (however inadequate the result) was never less than the utmost I could do; that I sacrificed other paid work and also much leisure by meeting Mike Smith's urgent plea for a weekly instead of a fortnightly piece; that I have never had one break or holiday, but filled the space every time. There was one column not used—Burns couldn't stomach the theme! But as old friends can, we survived the blazing row. Whatever the problems, I filed on time from wherever—Lae, Madang, you name it. Once in PNG I walked nearly three hours to get my copy to the nearest radio phone, but I got it in.' In all that time, Ryan claimed, not one member of the *Age* had ever said so much as 'nice piece', or even 'that was awful'.

When Paul Keating became Prime Minister of Australia in 1991 there was much about him that the *Age* columnist found unpalatable. Particularly some of his public language. In one column Ryan asked the question: 'What inner light guides the mind that bedraggles the dignity of his own

Parliament by calling Senators "swill" and "pansies"?' In another, Ryan noted 'the increasingly Napoleonic nuances that creep into the discourse of our Prime Minister'. These, he wrote, had begun with Keating's 'Placido Domingo of Australian politics' observation; there had also been the embarrassing 'Australia never had a great leader' statement.

But the column that went too far for the *Age*—and the Prime Minister—was the one in January 1993 that drew attention to Paul Keating's pig farm interests. Ryan would later say in his defence that all the questions he asked the PM were expressed politely; not one of them was of a character unreasonable to a man holding a high office of public trust. 'I was careful to make no accusations,' he continued, 'but simply to invite responses on matters of public interest.' None of this had helped Ryan's case. The *Age* published an apology to the Prime Minister; and the matter was considered (very seriously) in Sydney by senior executives of the Fairfax newspaper group which controlled the *Age* by then. Ryan told John Farquharson in an oral history interview for the Australian National Library: 'I was sacked at the request of the Prime Minister.' Well not exactly, it seems. Ryan and the *Age* editor (Alan Kohler) had never met, indeed spoken, until the offending column appeared. Many years later the ousted columnist put his departure in quite a different light: 'We had never met during the time I had been a contributor in high favour. I was determined to look him in the eye, even if it was for the first and last time. I shan't forget his expression when, eventually, I offered gently: "Would you like to end it?" I've seen the same look in a dog's eyes when someone stops kicking it. A short period of notice was agreed, and that was that.' One of those sorry to learn of the column's demise was Andrew Peacock MP, by this time Shadow Minister for Foreign Affairs. He wrote to Ryan: 'One of your last pleas was for us to re-invigorate our interest in Papua New Guinea. I concur.'

As it developed 1993 would prove to be a bizarre if memorable year in the life and times of Peter Ryan. After the drama—and loss—of *As I Please* he had quickly found a new outlet at the monthly magazine *Quadrant.* Before long he would be its 'favourite acerbic columnist'. In just his second contribution Ryan had stirred up a noisy, at times bitter, controversy and the intensity of feeling that followed seems to have taken him by surprise. The story that caused him so much trouble had begun: *'This essay is an overdue axe laid to the stalk of a tall poppy.'*

The 'tall poppy' was the historian Manning Clark and Ryan's former former lecturer and friend. Peter Ryan took the axe to both his professional reputation and his character. It was a beautifully written yet forensic and hurtful assault; arguably even an unnecessary one. Yet when the dust finally settled *none* of Ryan's key claims against Clark and his history had been refuted to his satisfaction.

Manning Clark's *A History of Australia* had been published by Melbourne University Press in six volumes between 1962 and 1987. Ryan was Director of the Press for the preparation and publishing of five of the six, but not the first, a fact that added an extra layer of controversy to the whole episode. Clark himself had been dead for more than two years when the essay appeared in the September 1993 edition of *Quadrant.* At more than 12,000 words there was certainly no shortage of material for critics—and supporters—of both parties to pick over. Ryan's assault was basically on two fronts: That Clark's *A History of Australia* was 'largely an imposition on Australian credulity—more plainly a fraud' and that the man himself was 'partly a mountebank'. It was explosive stuff.

Ryan had read the entire *History* several times and found all six volumes 'almost unbelievably prolix'. They were, he thought, 'a vast cauldron of very thin verbal soup, in which swim morsels of nourishing meat, widely spaced'. And he went on to lay out serious errors and 'libellous falsehoods' about earlier Australians. By the time volume six appeared he reckoned the *History* had become a construct 'spun from fairy floss and much of that false'.

All of this came with what could be described as a mighty *mea culpa* from Clark's accuser. 'Of the many things in my life upon which I must look back with shame,' he wrote, 'the chiefest [his word] is that of having been the publisher of Manning Clark's *A History of Australia*, and of having given him that support and encouragement an author expects of his publisher.' As each succeeding volume got worse than its predecessor Ryan said he should have followed his instinct and resigned from Melbourne University Press.

Admiring history academics quickly threw a cordon around their man Clark and hostilities got under way: Ryan was 'mad', one said; another that he was a 'cannibal'. In one of the more fanciful suggestions it was proposed that Ryan should return his superannuation to the University of Melbourne. Professor Paul Bourke at the Australian National University decided Ryan sounded increasingly like the authentic voice of the Australian 'knocker'. When Stuart Macintyre of the University of Melbourne said Ryan was a coward, he was invited to 'stand within arm's reach' the next time he repeated the claim. Michael Cannon wrote to Ryan when he heard this news: 'Please ask me along (with camera) if Stuart Macintyre accepts your invitation to fisticuffs.'

A stranger wrote to the offending columnist: 'The elegance of your writing and clarity of thought is in such stark contrast to the vulgar, intemperate abuse heaped on you by your detractors.' Another correspondent—this one a friend—had enjoyed Ryan's 'marvellous slap in the face of the intellectual establishment'. According to The *Australian Financial Review* the Ryan–Clark furore that had occupied the press for days was more like a sporting controversy than a debate about an academic's worth. Ryan himself was well aware that his conclusions would be unacceptable to many who read them. But as he later admitted: 'I took it for granted that contrary argument would be made within the arena of reasonable evidence and civil language. I never made a bigger mistake in my life.' The threats and the vile nature of some of the abuse that arrived in the mail also surprised him.

Support for Ryan was robust and—in many instances—more measured, a handful of senior academics and some old friends among this group. Writer and historian Paul Johnson joined the debate from London. Writing in the *Spectator* he described Manning Clark as 'the founder of the pom-bashing industry, at least in its modern pseudo-academic form'. Clark's work, he added, had been dealt a death blow from an unexpected quarter: the man who published it. Author and journalist Les Carlyon wrote a supportive letter to Ryan and followed up with an item in his *BRW* magazine column:

> What a pity Peter Ryan has become famous for attacking the late Manning Clark for his oddball history and windy prose. Ryan, the former Director of Melbourne University Press (Clark's publisher) should be famous for himself. There are few sweeter writers in this country. His political pieces have the toughness and clarity of Orwell; his musings on bush life have a perfection of form reminiscent of E.B. White.

One of the more intriguing commentaries on the Ryan–Clark affair was provided by the writer Gerard Henderson, Director of the Sydney Institute. Yes, he said, most of Ryan's belated criticisms were valid; but they were essentially 'old hat'. And yes, Clark was long-winded, his history close to fiction. In Henderson's view Manning Clark was 'the master of the leftist intelligentsia's universe'. The problem with *A History of Australia* was that 'so few (Peter Ryan included) were prepared to criticise Manning Clark'. This, he thought, could be largely explained with reference to the intellectual weakness of Australian conservatism.

The Ryan 'outburst' had come as no surprise to Clark's widow and in a statement published in the *Canberra Times* Dymphna Clark noted there had been 'earlier campaigns'. 'People could never be indifferent about him [Clark] and so it never comes as a surprise,' she said. The statement was restrained, even generous, about Ryan. It said in part:

> Of course I am sorry that he has launched an attack on Manning's *A History of Australia* but I don't believe that by going overboard with such a cantankerous piece he will diminish the stature of the work.
>
> He was a most able and energetic midwife, if you like, of Manning's major work. It is a pity that he seems to have found the task distasteful; and that he cannot remember it giving him any pleasure. But we continue to be grateful to him for his professional skill.

There was one delicious irony in the whole rumpus. It

had begun on the eve of an important publishing event at Melbourne University Press—the launch of a single-volume abridgment of Clark's history by Michael Cathcart. Great publicity. Great timing. 'We could not be happier,' an MUP spokesman said.

So why did Ryan do it? And who knew it was coming? The second question is the easy one to answer: hardly anyone knew. Of course the editor of *Quadrant*, Robert Manne did. He later explained: 'My motive was to encourage critical discussion of Clark's six-volume history.' The cartoonist and illustrator John Spooner knew because it was his portrait of Clark on the front of *Quadrant* that issue.

The only other person Ryan took into his confidence was his friend, the historian and author Geoffrey Serle. Ryan said Serle had encouraged him to proceed but was never shown a draft of the essay. When the *Quadrant* storm broke later on Serle had helped him to 'manage the enraged historians'.

Ryan's daughter, Sally Guerin, certainly didn't know. The first she heard of it—read of it actually—was when she was driving to work in the city early in the morning on Thursday 26 August 1993. An *Age* poster proclaiming MANNING CLARK'S WORK CANNED caught her eye. The word was out by the time she reached her office where the phone 'rang off the hook'. Her father phoned telling her to advise callers: 'I know nothing.' And of course she didn't. Maybe there had been a hint of what was to come in one of

Ryan's *As I Please* columns the previous year: 'Australians today, made uneasy by the shallow rubbishing of our real history, might reassure themselves by reflecting on the European roots and the classical continuity of almost everything we have—our language, our laws, our learning and our liberty.'

The impact and the intent of the essay once it was published are clear enough, though Ryan's motives are not. *Why did he really do it?* Why did he wait until Clark was dead before attacking him? We will never know or understand the cocktail of reasons that finally prompted Ryan to start penning his hatchet job (axe job actually) on Manning Clark. We do know some of the ingredients and there has been plenty of speculation about others.

The essay was not something cooked up once Manning Clark was dead, as the project was underway before its target died in May 1991. If we are to take Ryan at his word then one major ingredient was his need to 'clear' his conscience: to put the record straight about his 'shame' as publisher of *A History of Australia*. In a follow-up essay he had gone as far as to confess: 'If Manning Clark's *History* was an intellectual crime then I was an accomplice.' Ryan was very angry at the portrayal of his valued friend 'Mac' Ball in a volume of autobiography by Clark. It was a travesty, he said; an example of Clark's 'humbug'. It really upset him. It wasn't something he was likely to let go unpunished.

Did the essay also mark some kind of public service?

As Ryan told an interviewer well after the event: 'Historians let Clark get away with too much. His head got too big for his intellect. He'd have taken it as a compliment if someone had come along and nailed him up on a cross.' Public service or not, Ryan clearly saw the opportunity to make a major splash in Australia's 'History Wars', on the conservative side; and he had a sympathetic vehicle in *Quadrant*. Some of Ryan's critics accused him of jealousy. Perhaps they were right in some respect or other; but it seems unlikely. Why would a decorated veteran, the author of an acclaimed war memoir and a respected publisher be jealous of Manning Clark? They were both accomplished public men. Each on a different trajectory.

Whatever Ryan's reasons they had clearly been on his mind for years. Setting it all out had been a painful labour, he admitted, performed without relish and likely to cost him friendships. 'Perhaps it amounts to no more than having a bad tooth extracted, one which has been nagging for years. I am not sure.'

Ryan revisited the Clark episode in 2010 when he made a witty speech at the launch of *Final Proof*, his memoir of his Melbourne University Press years. It was called 'My Life as a Leper' and it outlined what he termed the 'doleful tale' set in train by his essay 17 years earlier. He remained unrepentant. 'You mustn't think that it depressed me as it unfolded,' he said. 'It had, indeed, an outrageous humour which frequently set me laughing aloud.'

One thing was clear as the Clark row subsided and maybe it was the *only* one: Peter Ryan had secured his future as a columnist. In a publishing sense a 'column' is simply a regular magazine, or newspaper, section devoted to a particular subject; or written by a particular person. Ryan's contentious views had already cost him two such outlets, both in newspapers. But this time there had been no such difficulty with *Quadrant*, well established as a political, cultural and literary journal; and (importantly in this particular case) conservative in outlook.

Ryan's future as a contributor was now assured in the form of a regular space, at the back of the magazine. Until his death, 20 years later, he would take up his pen, month after month, and produce in the end more than 200 essays. Eventually he stopped filing hand-written copy by fax. When the editorial operation of *Quadrant* moved to Sydney he switched to email, after making his first acquaintance with computers in his eighties. But right to the end the creation of the first draft of the column was done by hand. The magazine's deputy editor, George Thomas, handled Ryan's copy and later recalled that 'Peter on the phone was the same man as Peter the columnist: cheerful, wise and witty.' That column meant a great deal to Ryan, Thomas said. Once while walking to the Flemington post office Ryan had been knocked over by a car; he still made it to the post office and faxed his copy to *Quadrant*. He was about 80 at the time.

It helped Ryan that *Quadrant* applied no constraints on their columnist, leaving him free, as he would say, to range the world. Every column seems to have had the capacity to surprise. It might have been a gentle piece about the pleasure he derived from the company of his horse, Bonny, aged 27 (maybe older); perhaps the case for capital punishment in certain circumstances; or his good-natured frustration with Geoffrey Blainey after he had read *A Shorter History of Australia*. Ryan 'shut the book on the final page and went to bed, chagrined that there was not more'. He was a great admirer of Blainey's work and of the man himself. But as a class, he thought, writers were probably the most miserable bunch of whingers in the world. This revelation appeared in his essay, 'Ingrate Writers of Our Time'.

As if he didn't have enough to occupy him Ryan set up a small publishing venture of his own as a hobby. Rainy Creek Press produced *Crude Impieties*, a small book of verse by Sir Paul Hasluck and *The School in the Valley* by his brother-in-law Bruce Davidson. A small list certainly but one he was quite proud of.

Davidson was an agronomist and author of *The Northern Myth* which Ryan had published at Melbourne University Press in 1972. It was an important study of the physical and economic limits to agricultural and pastoral development in tropical Australia. His little Rainy Creek Press volume told the story of Tambo Crossing State School in Victoria. This was where it had all begun for Davidson and he remained convinced that one-room, one-teacher schools like Tambo Crossing were the best way to start an education.

By the time *Crude Impieties* was published Hasluck and Ryan were close friends. Sir Paul (1905–93), author, poet, career politician and for five years Governor-General of Australia, often stayed with the Ryans at Rainy Creek. (As the property was developed a house for guests had been built). Their association began with correspondence in 1959 about Ryan's former colleague Sergeant Major Kari but they did not meet until Ryan was Director of MUP and published several of Hasluck's books. 'I'd say that I regarded him as one of my very closest and treasured friends,' Ryan told one interviewer. There was one poem in *Crude Impieties* that particularly amused its publisher. This was a send-up by Hasluck of a fellow cabinet minister who was later briefly Prime Minister of Australia. As Ryan explained in a profile of his friend: 'Hasluck had composed its ten biting lines while cabinet was actually meeting; he slid the slip of paper across the table to Prime Minister Robert Menzies who was presiding—an excoriation of the odious William McMahon.'

Ryan kept needling away at the Clark issue whenever the opportunity presented itself and did so with gusto in a new book: *Lines of Fire: Manning Clark and Other Writings.* It appeared in 1997 providing readers with an accessible opportunity to examine all three of his Clark essays—the demolition job itself, his reaction to its reception a month later and finally 'The Charge of the Lightweight Brigade', a reflection on events one year on. *Lines of Fire* presented a broad sample of his best writing—wicked wit, elegant prose and thoughtful observation. Mac Ball was there and A.D. Hope, both of them in the *Men of Character* section. The book opened with the tense chapter in *Fear Drive My Feet* where Ryan and Captain Les Howlett were ambushed behind Japanese lines and Howlett killed.

At 80 Ryan recalibrated his life again. It was time to retire after 15 years at the Court, time to sell up country and city properties, time to 'settle down' in suburban Melbourne. But he did retain one link with the Supreme Court. After Sir John Young retired as Chief Justice the two of them met regularly for lunch until Sir John's death in 2008. They had become good friends since the day the Chief Justice had approved the appointment of the non-lawyer as Secretary of the Board of Examiners.

Of course the *Quadrant* and other freelance journalism activities would also continue, particularly book reviewing. Ryan had, for example, welcomed Les Carlyon's *Gallipoli*, describing it as 'a great big, rich, magic pudding of a book'. But he was not happy with a new biography of H.V. 'Doc' Evatt, published in 1994. It was, he thought, 'an ambitious book which yet fails a true understanding of a great and terrible Australian'. Ryan questioned the view that Evatt had been an 'architect' at the birth of the United Nations. Not so, said the reviewer. 'He was in fact one of the minor plumbing contractors on that job even though he did brandish his wrench a lot and bang loudly on the pipes.'

More than 60 years after his own war service Ryan produced a powerful defence of the American decision to use the atom bomb against the Japanese in 1945. It was published in the *Weekend Australian.* In it he argued the West must abandon feelings of guilt over what had been a necessary attack by the United States. 'As in advance, so in retreat,' he wrote of the Japanese forces, 'atrocity remained integral to Japan's military method. Thus were saved the lives of perhaps one million allied servicemen and certainly twice that number of Japanese soldiers and civilians … thus were rescued, just ahead of their intended murder, those of our POW's who had survived Japan's vile camps.' Quite late in his life Ryan's friend Creighton Burns also expressed a similar opinion. Burns had ended his World War Two service in the destroyer HMAS *Nepal* and spent five weeks on shore parties helping clear up the damage from conventional bombing in Yokohama. 'It was an horrific thing to have done,' Burns conceded. 'But I don't think it was a mistake.'

The final Ryan residence was a comfortable two-storey property with a well-groomed garden in Wilburton Parade, Balwyn North, about 15 kilometres east of the Melbourne CBD. This was 2003. Ryan's health was failing but he and Davey would live there for the best part of 12 years.

Peter Ryan had spent his whole life 'collecting' people. He once said the 'chief joy and enrichment' of that varied life had been his acquaintance with men and women whom he admired. *Brief Lives*, published in 2004, was a tribute to some of them and a mark of his own great capacity for friendship. There were profiles of 14 men and one woman. Ryan said that every one of them mattered to him 'as human individuals'.

The most affectionate piece, the first in the book and one of the longest, was devoted to Cyril Pearl. The two men had much in common and Ryan said there had been nobody in his life quite like Cyril for good sense, good manners and for gaiety. He also noted: 'With Cyril as with a tiger, if you twisted his tail you got bitten.' Who else does that sound like? The longest essay of them all profiled Ryan's old chief at DORCA during World War Two, Alf Conlon; the only woman in the book, also from that time, was Ida Leeson. Ryan credited her with 'resurrecting' his memoir *Fear Drive My Feet* 12 years after he wrote it. The poet A.D. Hope also makes an appearance. 'In the half-century that kindly fate gave me Alec as a friend I never heard him raise his voice.' So do Bill Ingram, the doorman at the Florentino in Melbourne, former Prime Minister Ben Chifley, Sir Paul Hasluck and, of course, Mac Ball. *Brief Lives* was one of the last books from Sydney publishers Duffy & Snellgrove.

From his mid-80s Peter Ryan's general health was showing the terrible toll that his wartime injuries and illnesses had taken. His feet (all that hard walking in New Guinea) and his back were 'gone' and mobility was becoming a major issue. He suffered malaria attacks right up till his death. In 2004 he had operations on both ears for severe skin cancers and a brain operation for a very large acoustic neuroma. (He was given five years to live but survived for another eleven.) Despite these difficulties he pressed on when he could. His publishing memoir *Final Proof* was released in 2010, a remarkable achievement given his reduced mobility and fast-deteriorating health. Ryan dedicated it to Davey. Revealing, witty in places, elegantly written throughout, this was his snapshot of a golden time in book publishing; a time for him that had ended more than 20 years earlier. Michael Cannon reckoned the memoir dealt with the great days of Australian publishing 'when objectivity was sacred and propaganda abhorred'. Quadrant Books, the publisher, said it offered a series of sparkling vignettes by the man who counted as blessed his twenty-six years as MUP's Director. A year later *Quadrant* published Ryan's last book. It was a collection of his essays in the magazine between 1994 and 2010 and appropriately titled *It Strikes Me.* As one notice observed: this was a remarkable range of essays reflecting an independence of view and a grace of style rare in Australian letters.

Despite a dramatic decline in his health in 2011—and a bad fall the following year—Ryan kept producing his *Quadrant* columns. In April 2015 Davey could no longer care for him at home and Peter moved to *The Connault*, a gracious retirement establishment in nearby Balwyn. It was a sprawling mansion set in attractive gardens and the new resident quickly charmed the staff. His daughter, Sally, said he was treated 'magnificently'. Ryan's desk was installed in his room, and he continued with his *Quadrant* columns and yet another relaunch of *Fear Drive My Feet.* But in August that year he was admitted to hospital, critically ill, and the family were told he was about to die. When the phone rang at home (was this the end?) it was actually Ryan calling. He wanted some reading material and he wanted to return to *The Connault* as soon as possible. Both requests were approved and back at his desk he produced a couple of columns. A major stroke felled him three months later. Peter's last words to Davey were: 'I have to get back to my desk.' Ryan had spent a great deal of profitable time at desks and had been working on his next column when the stroke occurred. It was going to be an attack on the Australian Republican Movement in the course of which he would be giving ARM chairman Peter FitzSimons a damn good seeing to (as Ryan might say). It was not finished but the handwritten draft was filed with his papers. Peter Allen Ryan died on 13 December 2015. He was 92.

POSTSCRIPT

Peter Ryan and Creighton Burns had an odd and unexplained agreement: they would not attend each other's funeral. Only one of them could honour the arrangement and Ryan did so when Burns died in 2008. Ryan had not only avoided his friend's funeral. When his turn came he actually missed his own interment. After he was cremated the family decided his ashes should be placed in his father's grave in Burwood Cemetery. Permission to open the grave was time-consuming and difficult. Arrangements were also made for the site to be restored, headstone cleaned, a new granite slab and a plaque placed to acknowledge the new arrival. Sally Guerin was surprised at what happened next. An email arrived with a picture of the refurbished grave and an invoice for the completed job. But her father's remains were still in their urn in a drawer of his desk back home in Balwyn North. It would take much more paperwork (and digging) before the man who never attended funerals was finally at rest.

APPENDICES

MY TALLEST ADVENTURE

'You say, Nichols, that in the North-West Mounted Police you were lucky to keep a whole skin.'

'Lucky indeed. Listen, Parker, while I tell you of escape by a hair's breadth.'

'I was out after a madman who had murdered his father, his mother, his two sisters and his brother. He did the crimes with an axe, the fingerprints upon which identified him as the guilty one. He led me an exciting chase all over the dominion, and finally, when he saw he was nearly overtaken, he made for the Alaskan border. Once crossed he was almost sure of a complete escape and I rode my hardest to beat him there.

'Madman or not, the man was a superb horseman, knowing exactly how to get the maximum from his horse, with the minimum of effort for it. The Alaskan border was only fifteen miles distant on the day of my escape, and I could, at times, just discern his figure on the horizon. He entered a rocky defile, his horse at the full gallop, and putting spurs to my own, I urged him to his greatest effort.

'I came to a straight stretch and he was no longer in sight. I knew what that meant. He was hidden to ambush me. Even as I was deliberating the best course of action, a rope whistled through the air and settled down over my shoulders. I was roughly dragged from my horse and hauled up a precipitous slope for about twenty feet. There I saw my man. With flaming eyes he drew his gun and forced me to march some hundreds of feet up the steep side of the ravine.

'"Stop!" he said when we reached a projecting ledge and he proceeded to tie me with his rope. By means of the spare end he tied me to a tree. There was still about ten feet of rope between me and the tree and I was like a dog on a chain. Suddenly he pushed me and I stumbled over the edge, and was left hanging in space.

'"Hey, Hey, Hey" he cackled, "you'll have time to ponder over your past" and with that he took a large magnifying glass from his saddle-bag and balanced it over the rope by means of two small stones. As the little yellow spot of the concentrated rays of the sun appeared on the ground s few inches from the rope, his devilish purpose became clear. Soon the sun would move around and the glass would burn the rope through. With a final taunt he went his clattering way down the path.

'The minutes seemed to crawl by, and as I thought of

the awful drop, sweat broke out in beads upon my forehead. I strained every nerve to free my hands but it was of no avail. Looking down I saw the man leaping below, thinking to make his way shorter. He was directly below me.

'Suddenly I felt the rope give a little. One strand had parted. Then another went. Only one was left. It gave! I felt myself hurtling down, down, down and that was all I remember.'

'And yet you're still alive?' asked Parker, open-mouthed.

'Yes' I said nonchalantly. 'They tell me I fell on the murderer—broke my fall, you know.'

Peter Ryan, aged 15, writing in the December 1938 edition of the Malvern Grammarian.

Evening By The Sea

The sun is slowly sinking
Beneath the silver sun,
And a fox is softly slinking
To his earth beneath a tree.
The barques of toiling fishermen
Sail safely home once more,
And anxious wives and children
Rejoice they're safe ashore.
And some sea-bird belated
Glides to her cliff-face nest,
To the gull that she has mated
And they spread their wings to rest.
A white capped wave, it shimmers,
And the surf sings all the while,
And the lap of a lighthouse glimmers,
From some far rocky isle.

Peter Ryan, aged 13, writing in the December 1936 edition of the Malvern Grammarian.

SELECTED SOURCES

1: SCHOLARSHIP BOY

Family papers held by Sally Guerin were particularly useful in tracking Peter Ryan's early life. So too were copies of the *Malvern Grammarian* magazine 1936–40, a testimonial letter (20/2/40) from Gordon Connell M.A. and Ryan's School Leaving Certificate—Class B, the University of Melbourne, February 1940. Ryan devoted a column in *Quadrant* (June 2013) to his old school. Kevin Childs spoke to Ryan about his childhood (and other matters) in compiling his book *A Month of Lunches,* Oxford University Press, 1964. Also helpful was the preface written by Ryan in October 2000 and published in the Text Classics edition of *Fear Drive My Feet* (2015). Dates, movements and promotions during their military service are noted, usually by hand, in official army records for Peter Allen Ryan, 1941–45 and for his father Emmett Francis Ryan, 1914–19. Peter Ryan's undated letter home was written at sea, between Townsville and Cairns about 6 March 1942.

2: COURAGE AND BETRAYAL

The most valuable insights into the World War 2 service of Peter Ryan were found in a major intelligence report he wrote after a three month patrol behind Japanese lines in 1943, a copy of which was in his personal papers; and in his acclaimed memoir

Fear Drive My Feet. On his return home from New Guinea Ryan joined the Directorate of Research and Civil Affairs. His service in that curious organisation—along with that of people like Alfred Conlon and John Kerr—is outlined in *The Backroom Boys* (2013) by Graeme Sligo. A profile of Conlon is the largest essay in Ryan's *Brief Lives* (2004). Other useful sources for the later part of Ryan's war service included *Scholars at War* (2012 edition), edited by Geoffrey Gray, Doug Munro and Christine Winter. Details of Japanese air raids and missions against Port Moresby can be found in *Pacific Wrecks* at www.pacificwrecks.com. Letters home from Peter Ryan on war service are held by his daughter Sally Guerin. His recollections of the sinking of the *Macdhui* were published in the *Age*, Melbourne 27 February 1988. There is a detailed entry on the life of Damien Parer in the *Australian Dictionary of Biography*, Volume 15, 2000 (MUP). Mike McCarthy's *Mountains of Ash* details the history of the sawmills and tramways of Warburton and district.

3: WINDING ROAD AHEAD

Some of the material for the early Ryan-Burns association and the immediate post-war years at the University of Melbourne is drawn from *Class Act: A life of Creighton Burns* (2012) by John Tidey. Ryan's security reports by the (former) Australian Security Service and the Australian Security Intelligence Organisation (ASIO) are available on-line. The best and most accessible profile of 'Mac' Ball is a memoir written by Ryan and published as a monograph by Melbourne University Press (1990). Ryan's views on religious practice can be found in his essay *Church Parade* which appeared in *Quadrant* in December 2008. The visit to Melbourne of Sergeant Major Kari was reported extensively in the press including the *Herald* in Melbourne (29 October 1959), the *Sun* in Melbourne (30 October 1959) and a full colour page feature and pictures in the *Australian Women's Weekly* (23 December 1959). The ICIANZ company newspaper *ICI Circle* (13 November 1959) included a picture story of its PR manager and his visitor from New Guinea. The 'Red Page' review of *Fear Drive My Feet* was in the *Bulletin* of 25 November 1959. The question asked in the Australian Senate after the publication of the book was on Notice Paper Number 20 (17 May 1960). The 'Spy' story by Ryan was in *Nation* magazine, 19 November 1960.

4: A REAL BOOKMAN

John Curtain's MA Thesis *The Development of Book Publishing in Australia* was submitted to Monash University in 1997, see pp. 56, 61. Peter Ryan's recollections of his 26 years at MUP can be found in his memoir *Final Proof* (2010). John Hetherington's major feature on MUP appeared in the *Age*, 6 April 1963. The shoplifting essay by Tony Thomas was published in *Quadrant*, 24 December 2015. John Poynter's views on Peter Ryan as Publisher appeared in *Quadrant*, March 2016. Ryan's Statutory Declaration when his war medals were stolen was signed on 22 March 1986. The recollections of three former Melbourne University Press employees—Sue Hardiman, Wendy Sutherland and Nick Walker—were very helpful in dealing with this part of Ryan's life. Ryan's End of the Dreamtime article was published in the *National Times on Sunday*, 30 November 1986. An article on Barbara Ramsden (1903–71) appeared in the *Australian Dictionary of Biography*, Volume 16, 2002 (MUP).

5: MUCH MORE TO DO

Ryan's three Manning Clark essays were published in *Quadrant* issues September and October 1993 and October 1994. Creighton Burns views on the bombing of Hiroshima and Nagasaki are on p. 31 of *Class Act: A life of Creighton Burns* (2012). John Farquharson spoke at length with Ryan about the Manning Clark incident in his oral history interview for the Australian National Library (2000). Rowan Callick's obituary of Peter Ryan was published in *The Australian*, 17 December 2015. Five tributes to Peter Ryan—Robert Murray, Geoffrey Blainey, John Poynter, B.J. Coman and George Thomas—appeared in the March 2016 edition of *Quadrant*.

WORKS BY PETER RYAN

Fear Drive My Feet
The Preparation of Manuscripts
Redmond Barry: A Colonial Life 1813–1880
William Macmahon Ball—A Memoir
Black Bonanza: A Landslide of Gold
Lines of Fire: Manning Clark & Other Writings
Brief Lives
Final Proof: Memoirs of a Publisher
It Strikes Me—Collected Essays 1994–2010

As General Editor

Encyclopaedia of Papua and New Guinea

INDEX

A History of Australia 44, 67, 88, 104, 105, 108

Allen Bequest Scholarship 7

Allied Intelligence Bureau (AIB) 18

Anti-Aircraft units 12, 13, 15

Asche, Austin 41

A Shorter History of Australia 113

As I Please column 101, 102, 104, 110

Atlas Publications 46, 47, 49, 50

Atomic Bomb 116

Australian Book Review 62

Australian Dictionary of Biography 67, 68, 69

Australian Financial Review 62, 82, 91, 106

Australian National University 92

Australian Naval and Military Expeditionary Force 4

Australian New Guinea Administrative Unit, ANGAU 18

Australian Republican Movement 119

Australian Security and Intelligence Organisation (ASIO) 41, 42, 49

Australian Security Organisation 41

Barry, Sir Redmond 73

Bellew, Jack 47

Black Bonanza 99

Blainey, Ann 75

Blainey, Geoffrey 53, 70, 71, 75, 91, 113

Blamey, General Thomas (Tom) 33, 35

Board of Examiners for Legal Practice 96, 98, 102, 115

Bourke, Paul 106

Boyd, Robin 8
Boy's Own Paper 4, 22
Brief Lives 34, 85, 117
Bruckner, Anna 62
Bulolo 30, 75, 86
Burnet, Sir Frank Macfarlane (Mac) 63, 76
Burns, Creighton 40, 41, 43, 46, 63, 69, 70, 75, 83, 85, 102, 116, 121
Bury, Leslie 35

Callick, Rowan 86, 101
Cambridge University Press 68
Cannon, Michael 72, 75, 85, 94, 106, 118
Captain Atom 47
Carlyon, Les 96, 107, 115
Cathcart, Michael 109
Caulfield Grammar School 7
Celtic Club 85
Chivasing 27, 28, 29, 36
Clark, C.M.H. (Manning) 43, 67, 104–112
Clark, Dymphna 108
Commonwealth Railways 1, 10

Conlon, Alfred (Alf) 31, 32, 33, 34, 35, 117
Connault, The 118, 119
Connell, Gordon (Cactus) 9,10,14,38, 88
Crawford, R.M (Max) 43
Crown Law Department (Victoria) 1, 11
Crude Impieties 113
Curtain, John 64

Dalkeith 49, 60
d'Alpuget, Blanche 80
Davidson, Bruce 113
Davidson, Gladys. See Ryan (Davey)
Deamer, Adrian 82
Directorate of Research and Civil Affairs (DORCA) 31, 32, 33, 34, 37, 41, 117
Downs, Ian 23
Duffy & Snellgrove 61, 117

Encyclopaedia of Papua and New Guinea 76
Ern Malley hoax 35
Evatt, Herbert Vere (Doc) 115

Farquharson, John 103
Fear Drive My Feet 39, 57, 59, 60, 61, 67, 82, 115, 117, 119
Final Proof 89, 111, 118
Fitzgerald, T.M. (Tom) 36, 57
Fitzpatrick, Kathleen 43
FitzSimons, Peter 119
Florentino 75, 79, 85
Frazier, Ted 30

Gibbs, Harry (later Sir Harry) 34
Glen Iris 2, 6, 12, 16, 58
George Watson Essay Prize 93
Gold Dust and Ashes 5
Griffiths, Bob 22
Grimwade, Sir Russell 73
Guerin, Sally (Ryan) 74, 76, 109, 121

Hardiman, Sue 71, 74
Hasluck, Sir Paul 59, 114, 117
Haupt, Robert, 92
Hazlitt, William 94
Henderson, Gerard 107, 108
Herring, Lt.General Edmund (Ned) 35
Hetherington, John, 67
History Wars 113
Hope, Alec 115, 117
Howlett, Les 27, 28, 29, 36, 115
Hughes, Frank 8, 11
Huon Peninsula 23, 24, 29

Imperial Chemical Industries 51, 52, 62
ICI House 52, 53, 54, 62
Idriess, Ion 5
Ingram, Bill 85, 117
It Strikes Me 118

James, Gwyn 64, 65, 69
Johnson, Paul 107

Kanga Force 20
Kari, Lance Corporal (later Sergeant Major) 23, 28, 29, 58, 59, 60, 100, 114
Keating, Paul 102, 103
Kemsley, Sir Alfred (Kem) 50, 60
Kerr, John (later Sir John) 34, 37, 98, 99
Kirkland's Post 22, 28
Kohler, Alan 103
Kokoda Front Line 17

Lae 15, 21, 22, 26, 27, 102
Land HQ School of Civil Affairs 37
Landy, John 8
Latin, The 75, 85, 98
Law Institute Journal 98
Leeson, Ida 34, 57–59, 117
Legge, John 34
Lines of Fire 114
Lumb, Harry 29

Macdhui 13,14,15,16,17
Macintyre, Stuart 106
Mackrell, Edwin Joseph 10
Macmahon Ball, William (Mac) 63, 65, 67, 85, 110, 115, 117
McCoppins Wine Bar 86

Malvern Grammar School 7, 88
Malvern Grammarian 7, 8
Manne, Robert 109
Markham River 22, 23, 27, 30, 35, 39
Mather, Arthur 47
McCauley, James 35
McLeod, Jock (John) 21, 23, 24
McMahon, William 114

Melbourne "Oyster" 82
Melbourne Savage Club 83, 86, 87
Melbourne "Spy"82
Mentioned in Dispatches (MID) 37

Melbourne University Press:
  Early history 64, 65
  The Ryan years 65–95
  Ryan management style 81
  Miegunyah bequest 73, 74

Menzies, Sir Robert 69, 74
Miegunyah Press, 73, 74
Military Medal (MM) 35
Mt Kare goldmine 100
Mt Tom Price 11
Munster, George 56, 57
Murdoch, Rupert 82
Nation magazine 55,56, 82
National Times on Sunday 92
New Guinea 2, 4, 5, 6, 18, 26, 30, 32, 33, 86
New Britain 32
New Guinea Volunteer Rifles 20
News Weekly 42, 82
Newton, Max 56, 62

Old White Hart Hotel 84
Oxford University Press 72

Papua 2, 6, 13,14, 15, 18, 34
Papua New Guinea 4, 6, 26, 75, 77, 83, 84, 100, 101, 102
Parer, Damien 17
Paton, Sir George 64, 97
Peacock, Andrew 77, 85, 104
Pearl, Cyril 48, 49, 56, 85, 117
Penglase, Nick 31
Perry, Warren 93
Pidgin English (Tok Pisin) 5, 19, 21, 38, 101
Pierce, Peter 61
Plimsoll, James 34
Port Moresby 13, 15 16, 19, 20, 23, 24, 30, 76, 84, 100
Poynter, John 73, 81, 87, 90
Pugh, Clifton 98
Quadrant magazine 9, 35, 68, 82, 99, 104, 105, 109, 112, 118, 119

Rainy Creek 77, 78
Rainy Creek Press 113
Ramsden, Barbara 66, 71, 76
Redmond Barry: A Colonial Life 73
Reed, John and Sunday 47
Romsey 77
Royal Australian Engineers (RAE) 12, 15
Ryan, Alice (Doreen) 2, 6, 17, 30
Ryan, Andrew 49, 50, 51, 74, 75, 86, 87
Ryan, Barry 3
Ryan, "Davey" (nee Davidson) 38, 44, 45, 50, 75, 84, 118, 119
Ryan, Emmett (Ted) 2, 3, 4, 5, 6, 121
Ryan, Francis 2

Ryan, Peter Allen:
Schooling 7, 8, 9, 10
War service 12, 13, 15 – 39
Decorations 35, 37
University student 42
Political candidate 42, 53
Comic book publisher 47–49
Advertising executive 50
PR manager, ICIANZ 51
Director, MUP 41, 65–95
Secretary, Board of Examiners 96, 115
Manning Clark incident 104–111
Books 130

Ryan, Phillip 3
Ryan, Sally (Guerin) 74, 75, 76, 109, 119, 121

Salamaua 15, 20
Santamaria, B.A. 75, 85
Serle, Geoffrey 88, 109
Sheehan, Mark 86
Singin Pasom (Papa Singin) 25, 26
Sligo, Graeme 33, 35
Smith, Mike 102
Society, The 75, 84
Spooner, John 109
Starling's Gap 39
Stewart, Harold 35
Suich, Max 57, 79, 80
Supreme Court of Victoria 2, 96, 115
Sutherland, Wendy 78

Tambo Crossing 38, 113
Teague, Bernard 97
The *Age* 82, 84, 90, 101, 103, 109
The *Australian* 82, 116
The Backroom Boys 33

The *Great Australian Bite* restaurant 87
The Insects of Australia 88
The Land Boomers 72
The Northern Myth 113
The Peaks of Lyell 70
The Preparation of Manuscripts 72
The *Sydney Morning Herald* 82
The Rush that never ended 70
The School in the Valley 113
The Tait Case 69, 70
Thomas, George 112
Thomas, Tony 69
Turnbull S.C (Clive) 41, 48.
Tooborac 77
Tuya 28

United Service Publicity (USP) 50, 51
University of Melbourne 11, 40, 43, 44, 64, 90, 91, 106

Wagang 28
Wain 24, 28, 29
Walker, Nick 79
Wau 20, 21, 75
Warburton 39
Webster, Elsie 89, 90
Whirlwinds in the Plain 90
White, Osmar 59, 60
Whitlam, E.G. (Gough) 83, 93, 98
Wilson, Harper 50
Wilson, Robert 50
Woodward, Edward (later Sir Edward) 41
Young, Sir John 97, 115

www.ingramcontent.com/pod-product-compliance
Ingram Content Group Australia Pty Ltd
76 Discovery Rd, Dandenong South VIC 3175, AU
AUHW021121060126
421769AU00004B/19

9 781922 454096